SO-AIV-093

How To Raise Happy, Loving, Emotionally Intelligent Kids

A Text and Workbook that Supports You in Rearing Peaceful, Happy, Joyful Kids

By: Tamyra Bourgeois, Ph.D

Smart Family Press
copyright © 1998, 2000 Tamyra Bourgeois

Revised Edition

All rights reserved. No part of this publication may be
reproduced, stored in a retrieval system, or transmitted, in
any form or by any means, electronic, mechanical,
photocopying, recording, or otherwise, without the prior
written permission of the copyright owner.

Dedication

To Matt and Claire - My most precious and beloved soul mates. Your exuberant, joyous and indomitable spirits bless each day of my life. I am honored and grateful for all you have taught me and continue to teach me about love and the joy of living.

My Deepest Gratitude

To four wonderful human beings, Susan Mitchell, Belinda Fruge, Shirley Russel and Mary Simmons who have all read this book in various stages of its development, and to my friend, Ron Sheets, for his computer expertise. Each one of these individuals has provided me with their own special insights and inspirations. Their efforts are greatly appreciated.

To my dear friend, Ernie Elsbury for his gentle but effective nudges that supported me in the publication of this book, and for his exceptional editorial skills - no detail was too small to outsmart his keen sense of observation.

Special Thanks

I want to give a special acknowledgment of heart felt appreciation to Drs. Art and Pamela Winkler, Dr. Ed Martin, Mr. Chuck Smith, and Dr. Stuart Heller who have inspired me with their wisdom and fervent beliefs about the power of the mind, body and spirit and about the infinitely creative power of language. They have each planted seeds in my soul that will long continue to foster my emotional and spiritual development. Thank you also to my late father Sidney, and to my mother Elaine Bourgeois, and to my husband's parents, Bernard and Maria Leerkes for providing me with wonderful examples and opportunities for personal, parental and professional growth.

The feeling of being valuable — "I am a valuable person" — is essential to mental health and is a cornerstone of self-discipline. It is a direct product of parental love. Such a conviction must be gained in childhood; it is extremely difficult to acquire it during adulthood. Conversely, when children have learned through the love of their parents to feel valuable, it is almost impossible for the vicissitudes (difficulties) of adulthood to destroy their spirit.

"The Road Less Traveled" - M. Scott Peck

Preface

As a student of behavioral science and mother of two young children, I have developed tremendous respect for the power of language. Inspired by the phenomenal insights I had gained through my own study of language and psychology, I began to share many of the insights that I received with others. I was then encouraged by clients, students and friends to further share what I learned by writing a book about the role that language plays in shaping the developing child.

In writing this book, my greatest wish is that those who read it will empower themselves with the remarkable tool of positive communication and go forth into the world inspiring children who are happy, healthy, and creative and who have what it takes to reach their full potential in life.

The following pages are also an effort at raising the level of consciousness of any adult who is in a position to influence the life of a child. Much of the text that follows has been written directly to parents, but teachers, ministers, day care providers and other influential adults can apply these principles to their individual situations as well. The reader can also apply these distinctions to his own emotional development.

I want to state here that this book is composed of my observations of the world around me, my many educational and self-developmental pursuits and my own experiences as a parent. I am not a world authority on the subject of child rearing. I speak to you as one parent to another. The material here is not the truth, light or way. It is my truth, a light and one way. What I offer you is a new set of distinctions that, if you so desire, you may add to your repertoire of parenting skills. Everything I have written in this book, I have experienced on a deeply personal level. I speak from my experience as a parent and as a human being. These principles and distinctions live for me and work for me and my family. I offer them to you with love and an ongoing commitment to create joy, peace and love in the world around me.

I will strive to simplify this text by dividing it into four parts -- all addressing different aspects of parenting language and how our language affects our children. (The four parts consist of moods, verbal, non-verbal and modeled language). I will provide many examples of positive and negative languaging and how they may affect the child. I will also share personal stories and observations that will assist you in making every conversation a meaningful and encouraging message for the children in your lives.

Lastly, I encourage you to work through all of the exercises that are introduced throughout this book. My experiences have led me to conclude that when we take the time to answer the questions, the learning experience is much richer and more deeply and firmly implanted within our consciousness.

Table of Contents

Your children are not your children.
They are the sons and daughters of Life's
longing for itself.
They come through you but not for you,
and though they are with you yet they belong
not to you.....
You strive to be like them, but seek not to
make them like you.
For life goes not backward nor tarries with yesterday.
You are the bows from which your children
as living arrows are sent forth.

"The Prophet" - Kahlil Gibran

Chapter 1

Rearing Healthy Children Through Conscious Parenting

Parenthood is the most important endeavor most of us will ever undertake in life, yet few of us feel adequately prepared for the magnitude of responsibility that accompanies the birth of our first child. Alvin Toffler wrote: *Parenthood remains the great preserve of the amateur.* What I hear in his statement is that even though most parents make a conscious decision to bring children into the world, fewer have consciously sought out the resources and distinctions that empower them to achieve excellence in the domain of parenthood.

When we take a historic look at the way children were reared, Toffler's statement is certainly accurate. Up until forty years ago, parent education primarily consisted of information that was passed down from one generation to the next. In the last several decades however, a transformation has been occurring in the way we care for children. A large number of individuals such as parents, teachers and child care providers are awakening to the fact that there is more to learn about child development than was provided through instinct, example and advice. As a result, many have actively sought out resources that enable them to provide excellent developmental opportunities for their children. By your interest in reading literature such as the information presented in this text, you too are among the relatively small but growing number of conscious parents who are seeking enlightened ways of rearing children. Actively seeking out the parenting skills that will serve children best is what I refer to as **conscious parent education.**

In contrast, parenting practices that were learned without our conscious awareness occur by way of **unconscious parent education.** I use the term unconscious to highlight the fact that these skills were not developed through conscious education, but evolved through our past and present exposure to societal child rearing norms and through the day to day experience of being parented ourselves. Even now, in an age where parents are eager to learn more empowering child rearing philosophies, we continue to use some of the ineffective parenting practices that were acquired through our years of conditioning. We continue to use these less effective practices, not because we choose to, but because these practices are often transparent or invisible to us. In short, we automatically or instinctively use the parenting skills that were pre-conditioned in our own early development -- they become second nature to us, and we are no longer "conscious" of them.

A certain amount of spontaneous parenting is healthy for the family when the interactions and conversations enable children to thrive and grow. The danger arises when parents unknowingly and consistently take actions that create barriers to healthy development. When parents do not give conscious thought to the actions and conversations they have with their children, they miss valuable opportunities to observe the effectiveness of their current child rearing practices. As a consequence, they also miss opportunities to invent new and effective ways of parenting, and miss many opportunities to acknowledge themselves for the fine work that they do with their children.

Becoming a conscious observer of the way in which we interact with our children is not as difficult as it might seem. You are actually doing so right now as you read this text. Parenting books such as these are designed to assist parents in developing a sense of awareness of current parenting practices, and are also designed to assist parents in taking new actions that are beneficial to healthy growth and development.

As you grow in awareness of your current parenting skills and practices, you will likely affirm that many of the conversations that you have and many of the actions you already take with your children are highly beneficial to their well-being. If you are like most of us, you will also discover that you unintentionally engage in conversations and actions that inhibit your children's opportunities for happiness and success. Even though there may be some sadness for you in the realization of lost opportunities, you can also rejoice in knowing that you are learning to consciously create new opportunities to inspire your children's healthy development.

The exercise on the following pages (as well as many of the ones throughout the book) is designed to assist you in bringing your parenting practices and attitudes to the forefront of your consciousness. Once these moods and practices are in your field of vision, you will be able to willfully and intentionally transform them in any way you choose. I highly encourage you to do these exercises in writing. They are very powerful and revealing. If you have an urge to skip one of the exercises, chances are, the exercise you want to skip is one that you might benefit from most. If you feel stuck on a particular question, write anything down. Sometimes the thoughts that we struggle to put down on paper, or the ones that come up after the initial wave of easy answers have been written, or the ones that come up only after a little coaxing or reflection are also the most revealing and helpful to us in our personal growth.

Exercise 1

Directions: Answer to the best of your recollection and understanding the following questions. Use more space than is provided if necessary.

A. The parenting skills I have acquired from my parents and society that are highly effective and serve my family well are:

 e.g. I give lots of physical love and affection
_____
_____
_____
_____
_____
_____
_____
_____
_____

B. The parenting skills I have acquired from my parents and society that are ineffective (in part or whole) and do not serve my family well are:

 e.g. yelling and screaming to make my point
_____
_____
_____
_____
_____
_____
_____
_____
_____

C. After reviewing the list in question (B) the actions I take with my children that I would like to eliminate are:

e.g. Scolding or shaming them when they are angry or sad.

_____

_____

_____

_____

_____

_____

D. I am willing to take the following actions right now in an effort to replace the ineffective actions and skills with ones that serve us better: (Check the ones that fit best)

List of Resources

_____ continue to read this book

_____ read other parenting or self-help books

_____ listen to parenting audio tapes or watch parenting video tapes

_____ watch parenting shows on PBS or the Family Channel

_____ consult or visit family community service centers such as the United Way

_____ consult family's pediatrician or child's school for further parenting references

_____ review the local paper for parenting classes offered by community colleges or other agencies

_____ attend parenting seminars, classes or workshops offered in my community

_____ consult a family counseling professional such as a child psychologist or social worker

Becoming a conscious parent is a wonderful awakening to the fact that your repertoire of parenting skills contains effective, as well as ineffective practices. Becoming a conscious parent empowers you to use your self-observations to address the re-occurring breakdowns in your current interactions with your children. It also enables you to replace ineffective practices with practices that promote well-being and happiness. Becoming a conscious parent also affords you the opportunity to use as resources other parents, friends and parent education experts whom you assess as competent in promoting healthy child development.

In this text, I will often refer to the terms *healthy child* and *healthy child development*. Since *healthy* can be interpreted in many different ways, I will offer several distinctions that define a healthy individual.

Individuals with healthy personalities possess the following qualities:
1. a deep sense of belonging or connection to others - healthy self-esteem
2. a happy, joyful and optimistic nature
3. an accepting, non-judgmental attitude toward others
4. a healthy level of confidence that does not breed over-importance
5. a deep respect for themselves, for others and for all living things
6. an unmistakable passion for life and a wellspring of joy and enthusiasm with others
7. an ability to speak honestly but respectfully to others about their emotions and moods
8. a high degree of dignity, integrity and honor
9. a compassionate nature that enables them to care deeply for the concerns of others
10. a sense of accountability and responsibility for all of their actions (whether the outcome is successful or not)

Conscious parents search for, select and consistently apply the skills that encourage children to develop the qualities I have listed above.

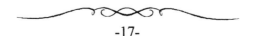

There are many essential skills and practices involved in rearing healthy, happy children. In this text, I will address the most fundamental of all: **How the verbal and non-verbal conversations between parent and child shape the child's personality and behavior.** By conversation, I mean more than the mere words we use. We actually braid language and mood together to form a conversation that is heard for its context, tone, body language, manner and inflection, as well as the actual words that are used. All of these aspects of conversation are what is heard by our children, and what is heard or experienced by our children has a most profound effect upon their lives.

In essence, our moods and resulting conversations are an essential part of our "being," and our children's "becoming." Most of us, however, are unable to objectively observe the way our day to day moods and conversations affect us and the world around us. Throughout this book, I will provide information, stories and examples designed to assist you in identifying your moods. You will learn to truly hear the conversations that you have with your children as well as the ones you have with yourself. This higher level of self-observation will empower you to discern which of your moods and resulting conversations promote healthy development and which may be obstructing you and your children from living the most joyful and meaningful lives possible.

In the next several chapters, I will specifically discuss ways in which you can design moods that set the context for healthy conversations and interactions with your children. Parents who rear healthy children are proficient at designing moods and conversations that promote peace, joy and ambition (the three main ingredients for a happy, healthy childhood and a productive, successful life). Let us now begin our journey into the profoundly creative nature of language by exploring mood and its role in child development.

Refrigerator Post-it

- Highly effective parenting can be learned through education, rigor and practice.
- Parents who stay conscious of how their moods, actions and words affect their children are *Conscious parents and are Parenting Consciously.*
- Parents who are not conscious or aware of how their moods, actions and words affect their children are *Unconscious Parents and are Parenting Unconsciously.*

Qualities of A Healthy Child

a deep sense of belonging or connection to the world
(healthy self-esteem)

a happy, joyful, optimistic nature

an accepting, non-judgmental attitude toward others

a healthy level of confidence that does not breed over-importance

a deep respect for themselves, for others, and for all living things

passion for life and joy and enthusiasm toward others

speak honestly but respectfully to others about their feelings

a high degree of dignity, integrity and honor

a compassionate nature that enables them to care deeply for the
concerns of others

a sense of accountability and responsibility for all of their actions

✄ ✄ ✄ Recommendation: Cut out these refrigerator Post-it pages at the end of each chapter and place them on the refrigerator or somewhere where you can review them daily.

*if a child is to keep his inborn
sense of wonder, he needs the companionship
of at least one adult who can share it,
rediscovering with him the joy, excitement
and mystery of the world we live in.*

Rachel Carson

Chapter 2

How Mood Shapes The Developing Individual

The Origin of Mood and Personality

We have all heard of the pessimist who perceived the glass as half empty, and the optimist who perceived the glass as half full. It is one's mood that causes the same event, a partial glass of water, to be seen differently by different individuals. Moods are physical and emotional states created by our internal conversations, biological events (such as physical pain or fatigue) and mood altering drugs (such as caffeine or sedatives.) For the purposes of this book, we will focus on moods that are created by internal conversations and how these conversations affect our parenting.

Moods that result from our inner conversations shape the beliefs and feelings we have about our children and the actions we take in parenting them. The moods in which we parent tend to have an undertone of joyfulness (optimism) or one of despair (pessimism). The same holds true for our pervasive life moods. We tend to view life as a joyful experience with boundless opportunities to grow and to learn, or we see life as a highly frustrating experience ridden with conflict and unresolvable problems.

One of the primary reasons why some of us experience joy in parenting while others do not, is because our parental attitudes or moods have been unconsciously conditioned through our past experiences. If we grew up in an environment where we felt cherished and respected, we have more than likely developed a deep and sincere appreciation for children. If on the other hand, we were reared in an environment where we felt somewhat undervalued, disrespected, and perhaps even disliked, there is a tendency to rear our children with a similar irreverence and in some cases, even contempt. For those who grew up in a healthier family environment, the bliss and satisfaction of parenthood will tend to come naturally and frequently. For the remainder of us, this joy and appreciation for our children is cultivated through education, insight and practice.

The inner conversations and moods that govern our parental philosophies also dictate how we speak and listen to our children. How we care for and speak to our children ultimately shapes our children's lives. Essentially, parents' moods, values, actions and language influence the choices children make as developing individuals and the actions and attitudes they select as adults.

Exercise 2

I feel that my pervasive life mood is one of _____.

I feel that my overall parenting mood is one of _____.

In answering the questions above, did you find any similarity between your pervasive life mood and your overall parenting mood? The profound influence that our life moods and day to day conversations have upon our children is widely recognized and acknowledged in the world of psychology, but my studies and personal experiences have made me aware of how few of us truly understand the power we possess in influencing children's personality traits, attitudes and decisions. Quite honestly, before I began my studies in psychology, I too assumed that children were born with their entire personalities intact. Though far from the truth, I held the belief that personality was hard-wired into our bodies. This was true for me, because I lacked the proper distinctions to challenge it.

Many parents were taught these same paradigms. (Paradigms are those opinions or beliefs which we hold as truth.) As a consequence of believing such a paradigm, parents are often driven to hold the child's genetic composition responsible for his actions and moods. Listen carefully and you will hear parents make statements such as, *He must have **inherited** his impatience from his mother.* Or *He must **get his temper** from the Irish side of the family.* The first statement infers that impatience lies deep within the child's genetic composition. The second statement insinuates that one could inherit temperament genes from an ancestor simply because he came from a particular culture -- a culture who manufactures individuals prone to ill temper.

Now, I do believe that heredity influences our thought processes, attitudes and temperaments. I also have a personal opinion that we may have all been sent to this world with certain personality traits that will serve us well in life. As a scientist, however, I agree with my colleagues who have researched and concluded that environmental factors do have a profound and lasting influence on an individual's personality and on the actions that he or she will take in the world.

Like any young living creature, children learn and grow through the moods, beliefs and actions that are generated by the world around them. The majority of our thoughts and actions are dictated by the moods, beliefs and examples that parents and other significant individuals communicate to us in crucial periods of our development or in vulnerable moments in our lives.

If we grew up in an environment of acceptance, peace, joy, love and enthusiasm, then our beliefs, actions and moods will reflect the mood from which we were reared. We will go through our lives gathering evidence to support that, on the whole, the world is a peaceful, joyful, loving place in which to live. The opposite is true if we were reared in environments filled with anger, degradation and frustration. We will likely but unconsciously spend our lives in a mood of resentment and resignation and will continue to gather evidence to support the belief that the world and our experiences in it are angering, dangerous, frustrating and unacceptable.

How Our Moods Become the Lens that Shape Our Vision
(mood and personality)

The predominant mood from which we were reared is often the mood from which we currently operate, and the mood from which we are operating dictates how we perceive any situation. This is often why two people have very different assessments about a shared physical experience. I witnessed a clear example of this several months ago at a party where I spent the evening interacting with two very different women. One of the women was my friend Sandy, and the other was a business colleague whom I will call Prisilla.

I assess Sandy as a fun, enthusiastic, happy and peaceful person. Her expressions, her tone, her actions and her conversations often create an atmosphere of excitement and happiness around her. I assess her pervasive moods to be moods of ambition, joy and peace. People are drawn to Sandy.

On the other hand, I assess Prisilla as having a very severe, angry presence in the world. My experience of Prisilla is that she does not seek out fun experiences, she lacks enthusiasm for play and she chooses conversations and bodily movements that express anger, apathy, victimization and discontent. I assess her pervasive moods as moods of resentment and resignation. Prisilla, by her own declaration, has few friends.

As Sandy, Prisilla and I stood talking at the party, we all nibbled from the trays of food that were presented to us. What I observed was that Sandy was complimentary of the food she chose and seemed to delight in the experience of eating. Prisilla on the other hand, criticized most of what she had chosen to eat and appeared to get progressively more dissatisfied with each tray of food offered to her.

After the dinner portion of the party was over, many people began to dance. Both of the women were encouraged by others to join a line dance. It was not surprising to discover that upon returning from the dance, Sandy assessed the dance as exciting and fun, while Prisilla made the declaration that the dance was complicated and exhausting. What became apparent to me, was that Sandy had spent her evening gathering evidence to support that the party was a joyful experience, while Prisilla kept herself occupied gathering evidence to the contrary. That night Sandy left the party declaring that the party had been fun while Prisilla left claiming that the party was a let down.

Considering my frequent interactions with both women, I have a strong sense that Sandy and Prisilla assessed the party in the same fashion that they assess most of life's experiences. I believe the rest of us do the same. We tend to go through life making assessments, engaging in conversations and taking actions based upon our pervasive moods. As a friend of mine says, *We all have our own unique set of lenses from which we view the world.* All of our lenses are indeed unique, but most of us either look through ones that are predominately rose in color or we look through ones that are colored gray. More often than not, the major crafters of these lenses were our parents and other significant adults who influenced our experiences and our moods with those of their own -- just as we are now influencing the experiences and moods of our children through the lenses in which we currently view the world.

As I make this last statement, I want to assure you that my observations about parents' moods and their effects on children are not intended to point a finger or cast blame. I truly believe that the vast majority of us do the best job we can with the information we have been given. I am clear that not one of us has ever awakened in the morning asking, "What can I do today that will help destroy my child's chances for success and happiness?" The examples of the harmful effects of negative language and unhealthy attitude presented in this book are provided with the sole intent of supporting you in your effort to empower yourself and your children with dynamic tools for living. Most importantly, these examples expose how unconscious some of our behaviors can be. It is only when these behaviors become conscious that we gain the power to choose differently.

Examples of positive and negative moods, the conversations that are communicated from the moods, and the influence language has upon children's actions and beliefs, have all been provided in order to assist you in developing a keen awareness of just how powerful mood and language can be. From these insights, you will learn to observe your own moods and actions and ultimately begin to use your observations to make powerful choices. You will also begin to design the moods in which you want to live, and you will learn to have the conversations that are most conducive to a healthy, happy life. With dedication, patience and consistency, your observations and new distinctions will bring forth profoundly joyous experiences in your life and in the lives of your children.

Exercise 3

1. As I recall them, the prominent moods in the home where I was reared were: _____

_____

_____

_____

_____

_____

2. I assess that the parent who most reflected my current parenting mood is my _____

3. I assess that my mother's pervasive mood was one of

_____

4. I assess that my father's pervasive mood was one of

_____

5. This is how my mother's most predominant mood made me feel as a child _____

_____

_____

_____

_____

_____

6. This is how my father's most predominant mood made me feel as a child _____

_____

_____

_____

_____

7. This is how the moods in my parent's home continue to influence me as an adult _____

_____

_____

_____

_____

8. This is how the moods in my parent's home continue to influence me as a parent: _____

_____

_____

_____

_____

_____

9. This is how I suspect that my children feel and are influenced by my pervasive parenting mood: _____

_____

_____

_____

_____

_____

In doing this exercise you may have gotten in touch with feelings that you had long forgotten or feelings that you never knew you had. I acknowledge you for being courageous and working through the exercise. If you are really committed to being the best parent that you can be, this exercise is very important to you.

When we do this exercise in my workshop some of the common feelings that come up are sadness, happiness, anger, joy, resentment, peace, longing and regret -- and there are more. Whatever came up for you, whatever you are experiencing right now, be accepting and peaceful with it. It is a feeling, an emotion and you have every right to feel the way you do at this current moment.

For those of you who experienced some anger, resentment, regret and sadness, please remember that your parents did the very best they knew how to do given their level of knowledge, education, family history and life's circumstances. If you were strongly provoked by this exercise, I encourage you to find a friend who is a good listener and speak to him or her about the emotions you experienced. Many of our feelings are released and "completed" when we speak them out loud to someone who cares about us.

The above exercise was not designed to blame or acknowledge our parents. It was designed to help you expose and become conscious of your own moods and where they might have originated. It is a commonly held belief in the field of psychology that insight (or understanding the origins of our feelings and behaviors) is ninety percent of the cure. So with that in mind let us proceed, knowing that this insight will empower you to make conscious choices in your parenting and in your life.

Parent/Child Moods

Consciously choosing the moods in which we parent is essential to the success of our children because moods and language, which converge in our conversations, do not simply affect our children -- **they become our children.** Children embody and design into their lives the beliefs and attitudes that we and other influential individuals communicate to them. As the quote from Rachel Carson at the beginning of the chapter suggests, when we live with a sense of passion, wonder and joy, our children will too. Conversely, if we live in a mood of resignation and resentment, then our children will likely adapt an attitude of resignation and resentment as well.

Some geneticists claim a child's inherent personality traits can impair an otherwise healthy family and negatively alter a parent's outlook on life. Based on my personal and professional experiences, I find this to be true in a fairly small percentage of situations. I believe, what one of my very wise professors often said: *It is uncommon that a highly functional person will arise from an unhealthy environment, but it is rare that a dysfunctional person arises from a healthy one.* The mood in which we parent and live has a profound effect upon our children's development, and parenting through moods of joy, ambition and gratitude are paramount to our children's happiness and success.

Before we go any further, I want to make clear that even though parenting in a positive mood is absolutely necessary for our children's healthy growth and development, sometimes emotions such as anger and frustration can actually inspire us to take helpful action upon a problem. In other words, what we tend to call "negative" moods such as anger or frustration can serve as healthy catalysts for needed change.

Throughout this book, I refer to some types of moods and emotions as "negative moods." What I want the reader to know is that in the context of this book, "negative" and "bad" are not the same. I do not believe that any emotion or feeling is bad or wrong. All moods and feelings are acceptable. Every mood in certain situations can serve to empower us. The key point here is to know when a mood is serving us and our children in a healthy way, and when it is not.

I often reassure my children of this concept with the following words: *All of your moods and feelings are acceptable, but not all of your actions are.* What I am reassuring them is that it is perfectly acceptable with me, and their right as a human being to feel what they feel, but their actions must be limited to those that do not hurt themselves or others.

There will, of course, be times when your "negative" moods (and actions that stem from those moods) will not serve you or your children in a helpful way. This happens in my own home more than I would like to admit. Even the most blissful unions between parent and child are colored with "unproductive" moods that occur in the day to day challenges of existence. What is important to remember is to temper our concern, frustration, anger and worry (all acceptable moods and feelings that appear in any parent's life) with an abundance of celebration, acceptance, patience and love.

In a later chapter, I will discuss ways in which we can design moods of joy and gratitude into our parental experience, but before we can consciously begin to design these moods, it is important that we gain a deeper understanding of how parents' moods influence those of the child.

How Parent's Moods Can Influence Children's Moods

Research done in the field of prenatal care has indicated that long before a child is born, a parent's moods may be influential in shaping the child's moods. I have a friend and colleague who is presently researching the correlation between pre-natal anxiety and the frequency of "colic" in infancy. Although her research is incomplete, she advised me that there is a positive correlation between the expectant mother's frequency of anxiety producing thoughts and the likelihood of "colic like symptoms" in her infant. Her work indicates that a significant percentage of mothers who were professionally assessed as having low levels of anxiety reported lower levels of "colic like symptoms" in their infants. Inversely, a large percentage of mothers who were assessed as having a high level of anxiety, reported higher than average levels of colic like symptoms in their infants.

This research suggests that a pregnant mother's moods and thoughts may have an affect on the newborn child's reactions to the world around him. In light of these findings, it certainly stands to reason that an alert and intuitive pre-schooler or school-aged child would be equally as affected by parental anxiety and attitude.

Although pervasively negative attitudes and chronic parental anxiety can and do have detrimental effects upon children's own moods and personality, the good news is that children are extremely resilient. If parents redesign negative or fearful messages into positive ones, then the children are not far behind with their own positive responses. I have seen many small but positive shifts in parent/child communication result in major positive shifts in the child's personality. In essence, a little bit goes a long way. Believe that your positive attitude, conversations and thoughts can and will have an affirmative effect on your children, and you have taken the first and most important step to making the affirmative changes occur.

Our Mood Cycles and How Children Learn from Them

Parents often ask me if I consistently maintain a joyful or positive attitude when interacting with my children, and whether or not we must sustain a perpetually cheerful attitude in order for our children to be happy and successful. To answer the first part of the question, had any of these parents seen me refereeing my children recently at the shopping mall, they would have probably thought I fell far short of the perfect parental role model. To answer the second part of the question: since frustration and anger are not pervasive moods from which I operate and rear my children, I do not believe that my frustrated mall mood caused my children permanent damage. At times like these when I am feeling stressed, overwhelmed or fatigued, I am much more likely to exhibit ineffective parenting skills than when I am ambitious, peaceful and alert. I do however, live most of my life in the moods of ambition and joy, and I believe that my children are developing ambitious and joyful personalities as well.

What I have finally come to realize is that my children will survive my moments of anger, frustration and overwhelm and that striving for parental perfection would only leave me more stressed and irritable. I am also learning to have compassion for myself. I accept the fact that I am a very *human* human-being, and my children may very well thrive better for having seen their mother making mistakes and occasionally operating out of ineffective moods. After all, they will have similar moods and experiences in life, so it is important that they see that someone they love and admire also experiences low moods but is not permanently consumed by them.

Essentially, our children will feel comfortable with their own mood cycles, by observing us successfully coping with our own. If we try to show up perfectly, we give little permission to our children to show up any other way. If we deny our moods, it makes it difficult for our children to be able to observe their own. Our children also trust us and bond with us more when we show up authentically and with vulnerability. When we allow ourselves to humbly admit our mistakes and express our genuine concerns and moods (be authentic) our children see us as lovably precious human beings rather than gods and goddesses.

In the section above, I have suggested that we strive to communicate to our children through positive moods, and that communicating to our children in negative moods can be beneficial as well. Although this may sound paradoxical, it is not. What I am offering is that we strive to interact with our children in positive moods, and we use the inevitable negative moods of human existence to teach our children how to identify and appropriately handle their own moods as they arise.

In the next chapter, I will bring forth distinctions about how to "appropriately" deal with our moods. We will discuss the importance of respectful communication and the importance of owning responsibility for our actions and attitudes. I am clear that when we learn to identify, understand and take responsibility for our moods, learn to communicate respectfully (no matter what our mood,) and strive to live as much of life as possible in positive moods, our children will surely grow in happy and healthy directions.

Refrigerator Post-it

- Moods shape our beliefs about parenting and our attitude toward our children

- We tend to parent in one of two moods - -joy or despair

- Children's moods, behaviors and beliefs are shaped by their parents and caregivers moods, behaviors and beliefs

- Children internalize what parents tell them about themselves and about the world

- Parent's occasional ineffective moods will not harm children but chronic "negative" moods may

- We tend to gather evidence to support our positive and negative beliefs - If we believe that we are having a bad day then we gather evidence that this is true -- often missing all the ways in which the day was going well for us. If we feel that our child is lazy then we continue to notice when he is acting lazy often ignoring the times when he is acting ambitiously.

God manifests himself in
the lovely things, the little things,
the beauty, the joy, the love
that occurs through patience,
kindness and gentleness -
In this children grow.

author unknown

Chapter 3

Designing a Positive Parenting Mood

The opportunity to parent is both a gift and a privilege. Children are not our possessions. They are unique individuals with whom the creator has entrusted to us. They are our temporary charges. Therefore creating a rich and nourishing environment in which children can grow is our gift back to God.

As I stated in the previous chapters, the most profound way in which we can contribute to the well-being of our children and to the world is to live in the moods of ambition, peace and passion. Through these moods, we naturally bestow upon our children healthy and well-grounded beliefs about themselves and the world around them. What often stems from these powerful moods are highly functional children (and eventually adults) whose actions and conversations come from a place of understanding, joy, passion and peace. Simply stated -- it is through our positive moods and language, that we inspire children to soar to the heights of human potential and to pass that gift on to the generations that follow.

How Our Moods Are Heard by Our Children

In the preceding chapter, I provided a brief working definition of moods. In order to create a foundation on which to build this chapter, I will expand upon that definition. Moods provide a context from which our conversations can take place. Our moods not only determine the kinds of conversations that are available to us but they also determine how we listen to others. In essence, the words we use, the tone we use, and the body language from which we speak all arise from the present mood from which we are operating.

More than any words we can speak, it is our moods that are heard most by our children (and other adults for that matter), and it is from these moods that children establish much of their identity and value in the world. It is said that the spoken work is heard as only

5% of what we say, and the mood in which we speak (including our body language) accounts for most of the remainder.

To assist in a deeper understanding of the consequences and results of mood, let's use an example that all parents can relate to: You have just arrived home from work or an outing, and you feel tired and irritable. Upon entering the door, one of your children approaches you enthusiastically and asks you to read a book to him. Operating from a mood of exhaustion and now guilt you sigh, run your fingers through your hair, slump forward and say in a resigned voice, "O.K., I guess I can read to you." What the child feels and hears is not the verbal acceptance of the invitation but the mood in which you speak, and as a child so often does, he blames himself for your mood. He has no idea that the mood occurred before you ever set foot in the house, and that it was not he who had caused it. What the child will likely assume is that your tired or frustrated mood occurred because he made a request for your valuable time. The irony is that you accepted his invitation, tired as you were, because you love him, yet he may come away from the situation feeling unlovable and alone.

Let me be clear that I am not suggesting parents only communicate or share time with their children when they are in a "good" mood. Sometimes children can be a great mood shifter in and of themselves. What is helpful in the development of your child's healthy self-image is that you share with them how you feel in the following ways:

1. observe your moods and the effects that your moods have upon your child, and share these insights with him,
2. as often as possible, converse and take action from a loving and respectful mood,
3. and regardless of your current mood, reassure your child that he is loved, cherished and responsible for his actions rather than your response to his actions. (Take responsibility for your moods so he can take responsibility for his.)

The Importance of Owning Responsibility for Your Moods

The concept of owning responsibility for your moods may be foreign to some of you - especially if you grew up in an environment where you were blamed for much of your parents' poor moods, or you saw those around you blame others or the condition of the world for what was wrong in their lives. The truth however, is that we are all solely responsible for the moods in which we live. Whether consciously, semi-consciously or unconsciously, we select our emotional responses. The situations we encounter and other people's actions can only provoke anger, sadness, happiness or excitement if we choose to allow ourselves to experience and express those moods.

Any of you who have been a spectator in the grandstands of a ball game have both participated in and observed this phenomenon. Have you ever noticed the reactions of the crowd around you? Isn't it amazing how there is always one individual sitting near you who shouts obscenities at the referees, coaches and players when events are not going as he would like? There is always another individual, rooting for the same team during the same play, who is cheering the team on with encouragement and enthusiasm. If you continue to look around, you will also note that there are other individuals who watch the game in a more quiet mood of enjoyment, while there are others still who seem emotionally unaltered by the entire event. What I am suggesting is that if we could not choose our emotional responses, then we would probably all be responding to the same situation in the same way. In the grandstands of life, the different responses occur, because people in resentful moods choose to act with anger, and people in ambitious and joyful moods choose to cheer.

Albert Ellis, the father of Rational Emotive Therapy and Founder of the Institute for Rational-Emotive Therapy in Manhattan puts this theory in an easy to understand form in his **ABC** approach to

managing our moods and redesigning our inner conversations. [1]
In his model:

A stands for the **Activating events** in our lives

B stands for the rational or irrational **Beliefs** we have about those events

C stands for the **Consequences** that we create because of our beliefs

In other words:

A is the situation. e.g. *My husband left me.*

B is the internal conversation we have about that situation. e.g.

(Irrational belief) *I must be a horrible and unlovable person for my husband to leave me. I will never find another person willing to put up with my defective self. Life is going to go down hill from here. All I can see is pain and suffering in my future.*

(Rational belief) *I am deeply sad because my husband chose to end our marriage. I am willing to take a closer look at the part* **we both** *contributed to the demise of our marriage so that I can learn from this difficult experience. That way if I choose to enter another relationship in the future, I can take new and more effective actions in an effort to make the relationship work well for both of us.*

C is the consequence of the internal conversation in part **B.**

---

[1] Albert Ellis, *A New Guide To Rational Living,*, (Hollywood: Wilshire Book Company, 1975)

Example of **C**:

(Irrational consequence to irrational belief in previous paragraph) Wife who is left continues to live in the mood of resentment for her husband, perhaps for other men in general and for herself. Because of her fear of rejection and low self-esteem, she is blinded to or outwardly rejects many potentially joyful and healthy experiences with men in the future.

(Rational consequence to rational belief in previous paragraph) Wife discovers that she and her husband both took actions in their marriage that eventually ended it. In a mood of peace and ambition, she eagerly seeks out and learns new ways of communicating and interacting in an intimate relationship. Out of her mood of ambition she seeks out new and exciting opportunities to establish a healthy relationship (or perhaps redesign her old one.)

This **ABC** model provides us with the opportunity to STOP and intervene at point **B.** When we are suffering or experiencing emotional upheaval, it is imperative to retrace our internal conversations and evaluate our current beliefs regarding point **A.** We must listen carefully for irrational thoughts and beliefs. If we do find our beliefs to be irrational, and we discover that they do not serve to make us peaceful and effective in our actions, then we always have the choice to redesign our inner conversations. We can redesign them so that they support us in creating a mood that enables us to take effective actions in the world. (Peaceful Consequences.)

Let us now bring this model to life with our parenting beliefs and actions.

Exercise 4
Using Dr. Ellis' ABC model above, complete the following exercise

Use a real experience that occurred in the last several weeks that made you angry, rageful, overwhelmed or resentful toward your children. This experience should be one where your child took a certain action that triggered an ineffective confrontation between the two of you or an ineffective action on your part.

Part 1
A (action that your child performed)

_____

_____

B (belief or internal conversation you had about that action)

_____

_____

C (consequence - what occurred after **A** and **B**)

_____

_____

Part 2

What new conversation could you have with yourself in part B to produce a different outcome in part C?

_____

_____

_____

What new actions or consequences or possibilities may have occurred because of those new conversations?

_____

_____

_____

Did you find the exercise above difficult or easy? For some of you it was probably easy, for many of us learning the art of intervening on our internal conversations and beliefs takes education. This type of mood and belief intervention can best be learned through counseling or by reading self help books on the subject of managing our emotions. Two excellent books on the subject are Dr. Ellis' *A New Guide to Rational Living*[2] and Dr. Wayne Dyer's best selling book *Your Erroneous Zones*[3]. These brilliant works by Dr. Ellis and Dr. Dyer will assist you in learning to consciously choose the moods and actions you want to take in the world. It will also become clear to you why in similar situations, some individuals consistently exhibit peace, caring, joy and compassion, while others experience anger, blame, resignation and resentment. I recommend both books to the majority of my clients and to my friends and family.

Though it is best to read Dr. Ellis and Dr. Dyer's books to achieve a thorough understanding of how we select and manage our moods, I will make one more distinction that will serve you in better understanding the phenomena of moods and emotional response. We choose our responses to any given situation (anger, acceptance, sadness, happiness) based on the internal conversations that are available to us in that situation -- internal conversations that were often fostered and encouraged throughout our developing years.

For example, rage (uncontrolled, unchecked anger) is often a mood based behavior that is passed down from one generation to the next. It often stems from a deeply ingrained teaching and subsequent conversation that others owe us, and that others should make our life as easy as possible - an easy life is owed to us. Therefore when others fail to live up to our expectations

---

[2] Albert Ellis, *A New Guide To Rational Living*, (Hollywood: Wilshire Book Company, 1975)

[3] Wayne Dyer, Your Erroneous Zones (New York: Funk and Wagnalls, 1976)

(what is owed to us), rage becomes easily available. Rage is the fuel that supports our belief that we are owed, and our needs have been flagrantly neglected. For example:

> *I'm boiling mad because my son did not do the chores that I requested of him. I don't deserve this kind of treatment. I get no respect. I give, and I give and I get nothing from him in return. He's such an ungrateful and lazy kid.*

On the other hand, if we learned early in our lives that we must each take responsibility for our own experiences and moods, and that we always have a choice as to how we respond, then we will rarely turn to blame and turn to rage less frequently when our children, other people or situations like the weather or the ball game fail to perform as we desire. If the parent in the above situation had responded out of this belief, then his internal conversation may have sounded more like:

> *I feel frustrated with my son right now. Today he failed to honor my request and did not do his chores. I plan to have a conversation with him about how important it is that he contribute to the family in this way. Life is much smoother and easier for everyone in this family when each of us does our part.*

In this example, the parent, though frustrated, is also accepting of the fact that his son will not always honor his requests or do so in a timely fashion. He also accepts the fact that the world will sometimes decline or ignore his requests or fail to honor his requests in the time frame that he desires. He knows that the option of declining requests is always available to us. However, by having a follow up conversation with his son, he does not become a victim. Instead he becomes a champion for his own right to be heard, and keeps his commitment as a parent to help his son understand the importance of taking care of others in the world around him.

When we look at the first example we hear a person who believes that others are responsible for his well-being. That the child *should* perform to the parent's satisfaction so that the parent can continue to be happy. People who have these beliefs will often get angry when others fail to live up to their spoken or unspoken expectations. They hold others responsible for their happiness and blame others for their sadness and disappointment. On some level, the angry parent told himself that he was owed certain things from his children, and that he could only be peaceful if he got them. This is similar thinking to the person at the ball game in the earlier example who got mad when he told himself that the team he was rooting for *should* have won in order to make him happy.

When we accept the fact that it is human nature for man to often look after his own needs and interests before another's, we may not be happy about it, but we live in more of a mood of peace and acceptance. When we learn to expect that situations don't always turn out as we desire, we allow the world and everyone in it to go about their business without a great deal of dissatisfaction for what occurs. When we accept our own responsibility for making our needs and requests known in a clear and caring manner, while understanding that the other person may still decline, then we live much of life in peace, contentment and happiness. Where our children are concerned, we will live in peace if we:

- make our requests clearly and lovingly known to them,
- remember to inform them of the benefits of honoring our requests as well as the consequences for declining them,
- and depending on the outcome, following through on the benefit or consequence (knowing that children will be children and often act first on their own behalf.)

Most of what I have spoken about in this chapter is the art of mood management. As parents we live more in peace and less in anger if we realize that our children are developing individuals and that they will learn only through time and a lot of patience to take care of the needs, requests and concerns of others. They will also learn to react to the situations in their lives with anger or in peace by observing the way you react to them and the world around them.

Taking Responsibility For Our Moods

I have a concern that some of what I have said in the last two chapters may be misinterpreted. In particular the part in the last paragraph where I state that our adult moods are often a product of our parent's moods. My fear is that some readers will take this statement as permission to blame their parents for the moods they find themselves in today. I have had to work with many clients on this very issue, and I have coached them all with the following advice: It is true that many of our moods and reactions have been influenced by our parents and by society; however, once we become adults, we have free will to choose the moods that serve us best in life and the freedom to choose our actions and reactions to any situation. If as adults we continue to blame our parents for our current situations, we disable ourselves and relinquish the power we all have and need to make effective choices in life. In light of this, what are we to do?

Regardless of their origins, in order to replace moods and actions that are not serving us with moods and actions that will serve us well, it is essential that we embrace the fact that we have freedom to choose, and that we accept responsibility for our moods and reactions in each situation that presents itself to us.

The way to raise children who grow up to take responsibility for their moods and actions is quite similar, and is as follows:

1. You must accept responsibility for your own moods and actions, and allow your children to hear you take that responsibility.

2. Consistently but kindly affirm to them that they are responsible for designing their own moods and for choosing the actions they take in the world. Inform them that the actions they choose will have either positive or negative consequences for them and for others.

3. Consciously choose to interact with your children in moods of peace, joy, ambition, confidence and gratitude. Your children will follow your example, and they will have learned that the moods mentioned above leave little room for blame and relegation of responsibility.

Again, it is impossible to be in a "good mood" all of the time. We are all justified in experiencing and responsibly expressing moods such as anger, sadness and frustration. Moreover, we need to experience the moods of sadness and anger in order to fully appreciate the moods of happiness and peace.

What every child needs is reassurance that you and he are capable of designing the vast majority of moods in which you want to live, and the actions you want to take in the world. In the inevitable situations where you both react in ways that are potentially harmful to yourselves or to others, learn to learn from those situations and design new moods that better serve you and to the world around you. Lastly, it is extremely important to your growth and self-esteem that you continue to see yourselves as precious and valuable and much greater than any isolated mood or action you can take.

To create peace and joy in the world and in our homes, no matter what our mood, we must make a valiant effort to consistently speak to others with respect and dignity, and teach our children to do the same. Maintaining a respectful tone and dignified use of language is more challenging to do when we are angry or frustrated, but every human being inherently deserves to be treated with respect and care. It is a birthright that many of us forget that we and others have. (Speaking respectfully is also a much more effective way of getting people to hear our concerns and requests than speaking from a mood of resentment.) What it takes to develop control of our moods and actions and to employ a consistently respectful way of communicating with others -- is awareness, observation, practice and continued commitment.

How to Teach Children that Their Actions Have Consequences

What if one of our children has taken an action that made negative emotions easily available to us? When my children are responsible for breakdowns in our home life such as hitting each other or procrastinating until everyone is late for church, I sometimes get angry. When I do get angry, I acknowledge my anger while striving to speak respectfully to them. I also explain how their actions make me feel and that what they've done has caused hardship for the family.

By claiming my anger and identifying the actions that caused the breakdown in the flow of our lives, I create a space for my children to learn to identify and deal with their own moods. This also affords them the opportunity to see that their actions sometimes result in breakdowns for others. This is important, because possessing the ability to identify our moods, observing the actions that trigger these moods, and possessing the ability to compassionately see how our actions affect others, are three crucial elements to healthy growth and development.

Furthermore, we must teach our children that although they are not responsible for the moods of others, they are responsible for coordinating actions in the world that will assist others in living life without unnecessary breakdowns. In teaching our children these principles, we teach them to have respect for others' rights. There is indeed a fine line between being responsible for others' moods, and being responsible for breakdowns that make it easy for others to respond from bad moods. As parents, we must strive to identify those boundaries for our children, and assist them in learning to negotiate within them.

In summary, when a child's behavior causes a breakdown, an effective approach to take is the following:

Effective Behavior Shaping Through Conversation

1. Identify the disruptive behavior.

2. Express your concerns about the behavior to your child in a respectful and firm way.

3. If you are angry, assure him that even though you have allowed his action to provoke angry feelings in you, you still love him and hold him as precious.

4. Identify the offensive actions as the cause of the breakdown, rather than the child himself. (e.g. *Paul, I feel hurt when you yell at me* - rather than: *I can't stand you when you yell.*)

5. Boost his self-confidence by declaring that you are confident that he will continue to learn the appropriate actions that will help him take better care in the future.

Essentially, you are reassuring your child that he is a good and loving individual who has taken a particular action that has caused hardship in the world around him. Again, this philosophy will help children to feel loved and will help them begin to observe and take responsibility for how their actions affect the world around them.

When disciplining my children, I often go one step further and express my love for them while communicating my concerns and requests. I might say: *Mommy loves you very much, and [use "and" rather than "but"] I feel angry because you took a dollar from my wallet without asking me first.* Or, *You are a very loving child, and you chose an unloving action by hitting your sister.* Using this phraseology in disciplining our children helps our children to continue to see themselves as worthy, beautiful, loving individuals, while also seeing that sometimes they make unloving choices or decisions that cause breakdowns in the flow of life. When these words are spoken in a loving and respectful context, they have a lasting and significantly positive impact on their developing self-esteem and in the way they take care of the world around them. This kind of conversation where you acknowledge the child's worth while isolating the inappropriate behavior also helps to prevent the child from making the *sweeping self-generalizations* that often plague us throughout our childhood and haunt us as adults. Sweeping self-generalizations are those assessments about ourselves that sound similar to the following:

- *I'm a bad person because I hurt Jim's feelings.*
- *I am a failure because I failed math.*
- *I'm a terrible mother because I hit my son.*
- *I'm a big loser because I lost my job.*

We do our children a great service when we teach them to see their behaviors as actions rather than reflections of their personal worth. When we consistently separate their actions from their worth, the likelihood of them falling into the negative self-generalization trap above is greatly diminished. They will likely grow to be well adjusted individuals who hold themselves worth much more than any of their individual actions.

In communicating our feelings, particularly when we are upset, humans tend to attack the "offender's" character. Attack usually begins with a "you" statement. *You are so dumb. You make me so angry.* What accusations such as these do is shut down communication between parties. The person being attacked is no longer present. His ego, having been wounded, has refused to allow him to listen any further. The person voicing the request or concern (we often call these complaints) no longer has an audience. Nothing is accomplished in this type of conversation - nothing except for angry, denial, hurt feelings and negative messages.

How can we break free of these negative assessments and character assassinations? We can begin with the following exercise:

Exercise 5

In this exercise, I'd like to examine step (d) from *Effective Behavioral Shaping Through Conversation* more closely. Step (d) is the part where we identify the breakdown or offense rather than identify the child himself as broken or offensive. In column A write a declaration that attacks the child's character. In column B, rewrite the declaration, addressing the behavior rather than attacking the child.

A	B
e.g. Clyde I can't believe you put the colored clothes to wash with the whites. You are such an idiot.	e.g. Clyde thank you for doing the laundry, and next time please wash the colored clothes apart from the whites.

I have spoken at length about the "how to's" and value of communicating positively and respectfully to your children. I realize that these actions may at first seem difficult to some of you, and to others, impossible. I want to reassure you that with rigor and practice, speaking with kindness and respect and designing effective moods for ourselves will become second nature. The benefits make the effort extremely worthwhile. Many individuals, have indeed created a way of being in the world that allows them to live most of life in the more positive moods of peace, joy, enthusiasm, passion and caring. Time and time again, I have seen this shift bring lasting peace, joy and happiness to individuals and to their families.

When parents continue to speak to their children with respect and kindness, their children will speak to them and the rest of the world with kindness and respect in return. If parents live the moods in which they want their children to live, then their children will observe them, emulate them and become living examples of their teachings.

In subsequent chapters, I will discuss more ways of learning to design moods that best serve parents, children and all of humanity. For now, I will leave you with one more example of how in the context of rearing children, you can quickly and easily shift out of an unproductive mood into one that produces joy and peace for you and your family.

Shifting Into Positive Parenting Moods

In the same scenario mentioned at the beginning of the chapter where you enter the house frustrated and tired, and your child requests that you read to him, you can quickly begin to make a mood shift by declaring something similar to the following: *Darling, I want you to know that I'm in a bad mood right now, but you did not put me in this mood. Something happened at work today that I feel angry about. I want you to know that even though I am in a bad mood, I still love you very much. I'll read to you after I have had a cup of tea and a warm bath. I think I will be feeling better by then.*

In declaring your mood to your child, owning responsibility for it, assuring him that you love him, committing to read to him later, and designing an action that will help you relax, (tea or a bath) you will automatically begin to make a shift to a more positive and effective mood. The shift becomes automatic or happens naturally, because when we can identify our moods, and make plans to take action to intervene on our moods, we feel in control of our own lives. This feeling of self-control is empowering and uplifting in and of itself. In fact, it is the foundation for the moods of peace and ambition.

Learning to take control of your life and your moods has tremendous benefits for you and your family. It truly can be as easy as declaring your mood, speaking your love, and taking an action that will shift you to a place of peace and perhaps even joy. Parenting from positive moods is paramount to our children's healthy sense-of-self and serves to assist our children in achieving all that life has to offer.

In closing, I would like to share with you an uplifting experience in my personal life that reassured me that working to maintain an attitude of joy and gratitude for my children is an asset to them, to me, and to others around us.

A couple years ago, I received one of the most wonderful compliments I have ever been given. It occurred one Monday afternoon when my son Matthew, then eight years of age, and I were sharing what we refer to as "special time." On Mondays, when my daughter practiced ballet, Matt and I would enjoy a little time alone. As long as his request was within reason, Matt would usually get to choose the outing.

On this particular afternoon, Matt chose to patronize our local frozen yogurt shop. As we sat eating our yogurt, Matt tried to engage me in several conversations before I realized how stressed and pre-occupied I was. Matt, who tends to be on the quiet side, becomes a very good conversationalist when he has my undivided attention, so once I became aware of my pre-occupation, I grounded myself in the conversation with him and didn't miss another precious moment of it. (I hold my conversations and my time with him as very precious, because I know that my reign as a central part of his universe is quickly coming to an end.) I seize every opportunity I can to be involved in his very interesting life.

Apparently, my enthusiastic mood shift toward Matt was evident to a woman sitting at the table next to us. Wearing a radiant smile, she came up to our table and asked: "Is this your son?" When I said yes, she replied, "It is so delightful to watch you two enjoying each other's company. It is a beautiful sight to see. You seem more like friends than like mother and son." Well at that moment, I beamed so brightly that one might have sworn she had just declared me winner of the lottery. By the look of pleasure and pride on Matt's face, I could tell that he also savored the compliment, as he winked this knowing little wink at me that appeared to say, "We are friends, aren't we Mommy?"

In my yogurt shop experience, I was exhibiting to the lady and to Matt my enthusiasm and joy for having the privilege and the honor of sharing time with this precious individual who I'm blessed to have as my son. My positive mood shift that day accounted for much more of my communication than did my words. If I had failed to establish or maintain eye contact with Matt, lacked interest in what he was saying because of a pre-occupation with other details in my life, or carried on the same verbal conversation without enthusiasm, then the joyful manner in which we were communicating would have been non-existent. What my conscious mood shift and genuine interest did manage to relay to both my child and the lady who witnessed it was; "Matt, you're important to me, I'm enjoying your company, and I'm interested in what you have to say." Since that day, I have made more of a conscious effort to remain alert in our conversations, more aware of my mood and to continue to treat my son and my daughter with the dignity and respect that I would my other good friends. For I firmly believe that a child can only truly feel loved and cherished in the world if he is genuinely cherished and appreciated by his parents and the other significant caregivers in his life.

Refrigerator Post-it

- Our children are not our possessions, though they are our responsibility. It is a privilege and an honor to be entrusted with their care.

- Our moods determine the kinds of conversations we speak and they determine how we listen to others.

- Children pay more attention to our moods than they do to anything we can say or do.

- When you are in a poor mood, let your child know why and assure him that you still love him and hold him as precious.

- We choose our response to any situation based on our internal conversations, which are based on our moods and past experiences.

- It is our responsibility as parents to kindly but firmly teach our children that they are accountable for their actions.

- It is our responsibility as parents to help our children learn to take actions that prevent unnecessary breakdowns in the world around them.

- When parents communicate their requests and concerns with respect and caring (rather than in anger or rage) children are likely to listen and respond in a positive way.

- When we speak our requests and concerns in anger or in an attacking, blaming manner, we damage our children's self-esteem. We also make it extremely difficult, if not impossible, for them to truly hear our requests.

I've found that worry and irritation
vanish into thin air the moment I open my mind
to the many blessings I possess.
Happiness comes when we stop complaining
and offer thanks for the good things we have

       E. Arthur Winkler, Ph.D

Chapter 4

Developing an Attitude
of Gratitude

Congratulations! You have already accomplished something that the majority of people do not. Statistics show that most individuals have stopped reading a book before chapter four. Proof that you are already committed to your children at a higher level. Pause for a moment and please acknowledge yourself for your perseverance and dedication to your family. Your children are blessed. Good work.

The first few chapters have prepared you for what I now consider the heart of the book, so let's get going. Shall we?

For the first couple of years as a parent, I gave much more attention (than I do now) to the difficulties of parenting two children. Thanks to my mother's excellent role modeling, I often enjoyed my parental duties and adored my children, but I had also convinced myself that parenting was often a burden. I don't think parenting back then was any more difficult than it is now, but upon reflection, I believe that my more negative attitude (a combination of past conditioning plus listening to a barrage of negative assessments about child rearing) affected my level of happiness as a parent. I was simply giving too much attention and power to the difficulties of parenting, and it was affecting my overall attitude about being a parent. My attitude was like a thin cloud cover partially obstructing my view of the sun. I could still see the sun, but it was not as brilliant as it could have been without the clouds.

It was a great day when I gained insight into the negative moods from which I often communicated, and this insight set me and my children free to reach a much higher level of happiness together. One particular revelation occurred during a preschool parenting class that I was attending. During this class, the instructor led the group through a guided imagery process - a day dream, so to speak, where we closed our eyes and brought to mind images of what the instructor was verbally describing to us. The process went as follows:

We first imagined ourselves walking into our children's rooms and finding their rooms a complete disaster. (This wasn't a very hard image for most of us to conjure up.) The instructor then suggested we observe any emotions such as frustration, anger and stress that might accompany the discovery of a messy room. After letting us stew in our emotional states awhile, she instructed us to walk into the room again. Here was the clincher.... She began to play the familiar song:

> *Where are you going my little one, my little one.*
> *Where are you going my baby, my love. Turn*
> *around and you're two. Turn around and you're*
> *four. Turn around and you're a woman walking*
> *out of my door.*

As she played this song, she had us envision the room completely neat and tidy, everything in order and in place. She then told us it would stay that way from now on, because our children had just left home for college. She then instructed us to be aware of whatever emotions were surfacing.

There was not a dry handkerchief in the room, and I don't think I was the only one to have a shift in mood. Since then, I have often sung this song as a wonderful reminder of just how special my children are to me, and how brief our time is together. There have even been times when I passed a messy room and smiled knowing it was evidence that my children were alive, well and with me still.

Below, I would like to share with you two of the most successful ways in which I continue to nurture a healthy parental attitude. I call this first exercise *A List of Blessings*. I began and continue to count my blessings in this way, because as the quote in the beginning of the chapter suggests: *Happiness comes when we stop complaining and offer thanks for the good things we have.* I know these are simple words, but I invite you to participate in this exercise so that you may experience for yourself what a transformational process this is.

Exercise 6 - A List of Blessings

You may first want to begin by finding a pen, a piece of paper and a relaxing quiet place where you can be alone to reflect upon some of the joyful experiences you have had with your children.   After a few moments of reflection, begin to make a list on your paper of as many of these joyful experiences as time will allow.

1. _____
2. _____
3. _____
4. _____
5. _____
6. _____
7. _____
8. _____
9. _____
10. _____
11. _____
12. _____
13. _____
14. _____

Though far from complete, my own first draft was quite extensive. It was a wonderfully uplifting list to behold.   There were many joyful experiences to recall in my day to day life as a mother; like the smell of my children's hair to the wonderful sound of uncontrollable belly laughter. Most of the list was comprised of simple pleasures like sharing graham crackers and hot herbal tea by the fire, watching my little girl's blond pony tail flop from side to side as she skipped to school and looking at the twinkle in my son's almost perfectly round hazel eyes when he is telling a tall tale. There were spectacular pleasures on my list as well, like family ski trips to the Rockies and drives through New England in the fall. All in all, it was the simple day to day pleasures that I listed with the most enthusiasm.

After you feel sufficiently complete with your list, you may then want to keep your list handy, and continue to list the joys and pleasures of parenthood as they arise in your family life over the next few weeks. You may even want to purchase an attractive journal in which you can record these experiences to share during quiet times with your family. I keep a blessing journal handy on the kitchen counter as both a reminder to look for these pleasurable experiences and for quick reference when I need an attitude adjustment.

When listing my own day to day observations, I continue to discover things I never realized were a source of joy for me - like the beauty of my son's smile, the warm and enthusiastic way my daughter answers the telephone, or the way I joyfully prepare an afternoon snack in anticipation of their arrival after school. I continue to have many revelations as I count my blessings, and I also feel grateful for having been enlightened and awakened to the abundance of joy that I have in my life.

For me, counting a blessing reaps even greater benefits than the momentary pleasure of the experience. Once I begin to hold something like my daughter's telephone greeting or my son's smile as a blessing, what happens is that every time I notice Claire answer the phone, or Matt smile, I am automatically reminded of how precious they are and how blessed I am to have them in my life. Over time, it becomes an automatic response, and the telephone greetings and smiles bring me to an instantaneous awareness of all the blessings that have been bestowed upon me.

Though I don't particularly recommend this second part, being the devil's advocate, I decided to weigh the pro's with the con's. I put aside my blessing list, and began a list of my parental grievances. After about a minute or two, I found that there was virtually no comparison. In comparing the two, I had at least five blessings for every one grievance. What I learned from writing the grievance list was that I had spent quite a bit of time and negative energy focusing on what really encompassed a very small part of my experience as a parent. Until I compared lists, I continued to gather evidence to support my claim that parenthood was more of a burden than it was a joy. In actuality, my overall day to day experience as a parent was pleasurable and fulfilling.

Having achieved this new perspective, I began to wonder why I dwelled so often upon the few frustrating aspects of parenting, while ignoring the pleasurable ones? What I discovered was that my grievances stemmed mainly from negative conditioning. I sense that some of you will find this true for yourself as well. In our society, it is all too accepted a practice to talk about parenting and one's children in a negative light. We see and hear it all the time -- in stores, in school, at playgrounds, even in church parking lots.

After writing my blessings list, I began to notice how many times I was "invited" by or had invited another parent to participate in a conversation where we talked about who had the roughest day, whose children were the most difficult, and which parental tasks were most unpleasant. What became obvious was that our society makes it more comfortable for us to talk about our difficulties than to share our joys. I feel that the time has come to put the difficulties of parenting in perspective and open our hearts and minds to the realization that **parenting is often a joyful experience**.

Counting or listing my blessings is a wonderful way in which I can continue to see parenting as the joy it really is. I think you too will find this practice most enlightening. If you are deeply rooted in the belief that parenthood is burdensome, I recommend that you put on your very best detective hat, and work diligently to produce evidence to the contrary. Hunt, fish and stalk for all the ways in which your children bring joy to your life and look for the many benefits you receive from parenting them. Many of these pleasures are very subtle, and are easily missed when we are pre-occupied, but they are there for all of us if we take the time to acknowledge them -- Pleasures like your child crawling into your lap for a hug, the sound of children's laughter, the sight of them engaging in a world of fantasy play, the picture they proudly and carefully colored for you, or the unsolicited "I love you" received when you tucked your child into bed at night. These are precious moments that can be treasured for a lifetime if we stop, look and listen for them.

I regret to say that like most parents, I all too often miss some of these simple but profound opportunities to rejoice and celebrate life with my children. When I do get a sense that I have become so self-absorbed that I have missed opportunities to enjoy my children, I quickly bring myself back to the present moment by remembering that my children are only here to enjoy for a very short while, yet my opportunities to consume myself in my thoughts, hobbies and career will be around forever. I encourage you, take a break from the hectic pace of day to day living and look for the pleasures of parenthood. Many of them will be quite obvious, but others will turn up in the least expected places.

When I first began my crusade for better parenting, I would consult my list often. I would even recommend that you make a few copies of your blessing list, as I did, and place them strategically around the house and workplace. With time, you will probably discover that you can maintain a healthy and optimistic parenting attitude for long periods of time without needing to consult or think about your list.

Although I don't consult my list as often, I have maintained a similar ritual of counting my blessings each night before I go to bed. The ritual I discuss below of counting my blessings before bedtime has been a wonderful way to end each day, and it eases my mind into a deep and restful sleep. No matter how challenging my day, when I remember to count my blessings at night, I am reminded of the many wonderful things that unfold in the course of any day -- I am clear that if I remember to look for them, even my most trying days have their precious moments of joy.

A Prayer of Gratitude

It is my personal and professional experience that this next process has a profoundly positive effect on the way we interact with our children and on the way we view our lives. It is yet another simple but profound way we can evoke joy and gratitude for all the beauty and wonder that surrounds us. This is how the process works best for me:

Upon retiring each night, I prop up my pillows and sit up for a minute or two in bed. I sit, because when my head hits the pillow, I am instantaneously asleep. I then reflect upon my day and recall ten pleasurable experiences or things that have occurred for which I am grateful - like the way a neighbor may have assisted me in time of need or my admiration for a rose that bloomed in my garden that day. Usually a good fifty percent include situations with my children. Often I recall little things like a joke they've told or the way one of them has snuggled next to me while we read a book together. This exercise instantly evokes peace and joy in me, because it brings me back to a sense of gratitude for all that life has to offer.

One client to whom I recommended the practice, informed me that she purchased a similar journal to the one I recommended earlier, and upon retiring for the evening, she dates and lists ten things that occurred during her day for which she is thankful. She shared with me that she plans to give a copy of the journal to each of her three children when they leave home to begin their adult lives. Her story touched me deeply. I'm sure the journal will someday be treasured by her children as an affirmation of how precious she held her relationship with them and the joyful way in which she chose to live her life.

Exercise 7

Tonight upon going to bed use the space below or your own special notebook or journal to list ten blessings and special moments that you recall from your day. (be sure to include your children in several of these.)

1. _____
2. _____
3. _____
4. _____
5. _____
6. _____
7. _____
8. _____
9. _____
10. _____
11. _____
12. _____
13. _____
14. _____

On days when I feel my parenting skills are not at their best and my insecurities still lingering, I remember to include in my list a few things that I did well as a parent. This allows me to see myself as the blessing that I am, rather than belittle myself for my human errors. I highly recommend this practice of counterbalancing the little, not so good we have done with lots of recollections of the good things that we have accomplished for ourselves and for others. Acknowledging ourselves for our accomplishments is healthy, it is wise and it is the self-compassion that we need to continue to thrive and develop as parents and as individuals. I apply this "Count my blessing ritual" not only with my parenting, but when I feel like a less than perfect wife, friend, daughter or employee too. I do spend time reflecting on and learning from my mistakes, but I close with the things I have done well. I do so because it shifts me to a more peaceful mood where I return to the larger good of who I am, rather than define myself by the ways in which I may have faltered.

There is a parenting and teaching slogan that states: "Catch your child doing something good," so when counting your blessings, remember to catch yourself doing something well also. Taking time each night to honor yourself and your contributions to the world will not only continue to build your own self-esteem, but will also assist your children in developing a healthy level of self-esteem and self-appreciation as well. You see, one way they learn self-acceptance and self-appreciation is by watching how you care for and love yourself. I also have a personal and spiritual belief that each time we remember to thank heaven for what we have, we are thanked in return with more and more blessings.

I can't begin to tell you how often this count your blessing ritual has served to pull me out of a deep hole I have dug for myself. On many occasions, my mood has shifted to an even higher level than it ever was before. For example, I volunteer some of my time for a charitable organization, and earlier this year, I made a mistake when booking someone to speak at our conference. The mistake caused hardship for the person who had committed to a different time than I inadvertently scheduled. Since we had already advertised this event, I had to replace the speaker with someone else. I felt incompetent and angry with myself and embarrassed about my oversight.

For at least thirty of the forty minutes it took me to drive home on the day I discovered my mistake, I mentally beat myself black and blue for my lack of attentiveness to detail. Battle fatigue began to set in and I even started to feel guilty for having chastised myself so severely. Finally I remembered how uplifted I usually felt when I count my blessings, so I did just that. For the remainder of the ride home, I recalled all the really good things I have done for this organization, and before long, I felt confident and happy again.

Whether at bedtime, upon awakening or when the need arises, I highly recommend the practice of counting your blessings and acknowledging yourself for the good things that you do for your children and for the world around you. You may want to teach your children how to count their blessings as well. It can even be a family ritual -- perhaps at dinner or before going to bed. Though I find myself counting my blessings often, I also find it necessary to establish a time each day for blessings and acknowledgments so that I can keep the ritual alive. It aids me and my family in maintaining an attitude of gratitude that is essential to an overall attitude of peace, love and harmony in our home.

Gratitude is essential to a happy family, and as I stated in the previous chapter, to serve our children well, our repertoire of moods will also include compassion, joy, optimism, inner peace and love. By allowing ourselves to see and focus on the joyous experiences in our lives, we make happiness, peace and harmony a frequent way of living in the world.

In the last part of this chapter, I will provide you with additional methods for shifting from moods that are not serving you and your family, to moods that create an atmosphere of love and appreciation. As with the blessing list and the prayer of gratitude, I have often used the mood enhancers that I list below to transform moods of irritation and overwhelm into moods of inner-peace and joy.

When we learn to successfully re-design our moods, we give ourselves and our families a most precious gift of love -- For in learning to hurdle our emotional obstacles in this way, we continually create a space for self-fulfillment to emerge. Our children will inherit this same quality and together you will fill your lives with joy and prosperity.

I want to preface this list of ways to shift moods with the following qualification: There are appropriate times to shift moods and there are times when it is healthy and helpful to remain in a current mood in order to learn and to grow. Sometimes moods of anger can be productive in helping us to take righteous action, and moods of grief and sadness can be productive in working through loss. There are many times when our "uncomfortable" or "painful" moods are a bridge to learning, but there are other times when they become barriers to successful living. It is in the latter situation that we will benefit by re-designing our moods with one of the aforementioned exercises or the techniques that follow.

1. **Deep Relaxation/Meditation**: There are many wonderful books, tapes and resources to assist us in learning to relax our bodies and quiet the unproductive or stressful chatter that trouble our minds. Most colleges and communities offer classes in meditation or relaxation training. Personally speaking, meditation is the most powerful tool I have, not only in helping me to shift moods, but in helping me to maintain a peaceful mood all day.

Meditation and deep relaxation have a profoundly tranquil effect on my body and my mind. Meditation helps quiet my thoughts, eases the tension in my body and it interrupts the patterns of negative thinking. I prefer to meditate at least thirty minutes per day, but even five minutes of deep relaxation is often enough to shift my mood into a more peaceful one. I have experienced such profound tranquillity in meditation that I now consider it a necessity, like eating, rather than a luxury to afford myself when I can "spare" the time.

I have discovered that the times when I "think" I have the least amount of time to meditate, are the times I need meditation most. When I feel myself harried or stressed, I stop what I am doing and take a break to relax and clear my mind. Depending on my time constraints, I may relax for just a minute or two or deeply relax for twenty to thirty. No matter how short or long a time I have spent relaxing, the resulting mood shift is always worth the effort it took to interrupt my hectic schedule and break the chain of stress. I directly attribute meditation to my excellent health and my positive attitude. I encourage you to explore what can transpire in your own life through the art of profound relaxation.

2. **Celebrations on ordinary days**: We are creatures of habit and though this serves us well at times, our daily routines often leave little room for family fun and the spontaneous joy of living. My family and I have learned to celebrate life on ordinary days by having picnics in the park after school or a picnic dinner in the living room on a cold winter's night. On weekday nights, we sometimes rent videos, complete with a bowl of popcorn, or light a fire and drink cocoa or herbal tea. We have gone on early morning nature hikes in the back yard before school and celebrate lost teeth with cake and ice-cream. One of my favorite special-ordinary day activities is donning our pajamas and having the entire family cuddle in my king sized bed for story and reading time.

As adults, we often consider it a luxury to celebrate life, but our children make it a priority to joyfully partake in the host of simple pleasures that surround us. As I come to appreciate this quality more and more, I am also learning to listen and learn from my children by attending to their actions and the requests they make of me.

While working feverishly on my computer the other day, my son asked me to swing with him on the hammock. My initial reaction was, as it often is, to tell him that "I'd love to join him, but that I was busy." On that day however, I remembered the advice I have given many, and I reluctantly tore myself away from my work to join him on the hammock. It was a beautiful spring afternoon, and after the minute or two that I needed to relax my body and quiet my mind, I began to experience the sheer bliss of peaceful and inactive enjoyment of life. He and I laid on the hammock for quite some time, and I left our experience feeling rejuvenated, peaceful and emotionally connected on a deeper level. I thanked him for helping me take the opportunity to celebrate such a gorgeous spring day, and I requested that he help me do this more in the future. He gladly agreed.

My children often request that I partake in leisurely pursuits with them, but I must admit, I often convince myself that what I am doing at the time (dishes, laundry, computer work...) is more important. When I do take these breaks from the normal, hectic pace of my life and celebrate simple pleasures such as swinging on the hammock with Matt or sharing conversations with Claire over a cup of tea, I never regret them. I am clear that when I am ready to leave this world, I will never say, *I regret not spending more time doing the dishes or at the office.* I do sense however, I would regret not taking opportunities to be with my children and to enjoy the richness that the simple pleasures of life have to offer me. I often use the following thought as a check in: *In fifty years, am I more likely to regret not doing the dishes tonight, or not celebrating this moment with my child?* It is a very powerful priority setter.

Kathy Johnston, a school guidance counselor and friend, recently gave me a poem that expresses my sentiments perfectly:

Dishes and scrubbing can wait till tomorrow
For babies grow up, I've learned to my sorrow
So quiet down cobwebs; dust go to sleep
I'm rocking my baby and babies don't keep.
author unknown

There are numerous ways you can create a mood of peace and joyful celebration on days that would otherwise fall by the wayside of routine. You can follow the spontaneous lead of your highly creative children and partake in activities that you can do together. You can read books and magazines such as *Family Fun* that help inspire creative ideas, or you can do special things for yourself like take a break in the middle of the day to read a novel or take a warm bath with candles as a way of unwinding in the evening. Pleasure and enjoyment of life should not be reserved for times when all the "necessary stuff" has been handled. Pleasure and enjoyment should be an essential part of the "necessary stuff" that makes life worth living!

3. **Talk to Someone:** Another excellent way to shift moods is by talking to someone who is a "good listener" for you. It's important that the person is a good listener, because people who are not, can inadvertently assist us in deepening our negative moods. A good listener possesses the following qualities:

- Attends to what you are saying (is not distracted easily)
- Lets you complete your thoughts without interruption
- Does not give advice unless he asks your permission to do so

- Is accepting and compassionate rather than judgmental and moral
- Does not project his needs, desires, standards and ethics upon your situation unless you invite him to do so.
- Does not turn your conversation into a conversation focused on his own needs (e.g. Oh! you think you have it bad, I've ....)

In addition, a good listener is someone whose listening allows us to see solutions or alternatives to problems and creates a space for us to learn and grow. A good listener helps us to identify and gain clarity about our feelings and moods. A good listener is easily distinguished from others, because we often come away from the conversation feeling rejuvenated and ambitious and feeling good about ourselves as well.

4. **Journaling**: Similar to having a conversation with someone, journaling is a way for us to speak and clarify our thoughts. A friend of mind speaks of the thoughts we have that are never spoken or written but continue to plague us as: "thoughts churning in the endless tunnels of our minds." I have had this experience. I will unproductively obsess about something over and over in my mind, until I finally speak it to someone or write about it. In the process of speaking or writing about my difficulty, the solution seems to become clear and the problem or mood diminishes. Clarity occurs because it is through the process of speaking or writing that we are called to make sense of our thoughts. In other words, as long as we keep our ideas churning abstractly in the tunnels of our minds, we are not compelled to make sense of them. They remain unclear to us. However, when we commit ourselves to speak or write about our concerns, we find that we must do so in a coherent fashion. What often results is a coherent look at what is bothering us. Once clear, situations and moods are much easier to work with and resolve than when they remain in the recesses of our minds. It has been my

professional and personal experience that mood shifts often occur while we are writing or in conversation about our feelings, emotions and difficulties.

Automatic writing is a method whereby you sit down with paper and a pencil and continue for a designated period to write about your experience without stopping. Even in periods that you are at a loss for words, you continue to write your thoughts. You can, for example, say: *as I sit here writing, I cannot think of anything else to say, but I am going to continue to write until something else arises.....* What often transpires is a creative breakthrough that allows us to work through the unconscious obstacles we have created to avoid change.

5. **Music**: Music has been used to inspire mood shifts since the dawn of man. Primitive cultures knew the power of the drum to inspire their warriors to battle. Recently a 40,000 year old flute, carved from a leg bone of a bear by Neanderthals, was found near Slovenia[4] - perhaps used to inspire Neanderthal man to a sense of peace and tranquillity. Like your primitive ancestors, I would like to encourage you to experiment with music. Listen to a variety of styles and see which moods are inspired within you.

There is music written especially to calm us down and music written in an effort to motivate us into movement and action. In a motivation class that I attended last year, we paired up and made a tape for each other. One side was inspiring and invigorating and the other side was relaxing and tranquil. When I need to shift my mood one way or the other, I often listen to one side or the other of the tape I produced or the tape that was recorded for me. It has often succeeded in producing the mood that I am striving to achieve. You might consider recording a similar tape for yourself and see how truly effective music can be in helping you design the mood that serves you best at the moment. You can play the motivational side in the car while going to work in the morning or

---

[4] National Geographic Magazine, Vol. 192, No.3 September 1997

to inspire your children to do their chores. You can also play the relaxing side on the way home from work, in the middle of a hectic day or when you think your children could use a little calming down. Music truly works wonders to soothe the savage beast and to inspire the sluggish one.

6. **Movement**: Movement is an excellent way to sJ.ift moods. Movement work such as dance and physical exercise can quickly energize us (sometimes to a state of euphoria) and the more tranquil and melodic rhythm of slow dance and quieter exercises such as yoga or Tai-Chi can help to calm our bodies down. How many times have we come home tired, not wanting to jog, walk or go to exercise class, then once we pushed ourselves into doing it, we began to feel invigorated with boundless energy way into the evening? There are some physiological reasons why this occurs, but feeling tired is also a mood rather than a physical state like sleepiness. Therefore, when we shift our mood into one of ambition, the "tired mood" goes away.

When I am tired, one of my favorite mood shifters is to roller blade in my neighborhood while playing the inspirational side of one of my tapes. Perhaps because I am getting a double dose of moo⟨! shifters (music and exercise) it has been a foolproof way of lifting me into a peaceful yet ambitious and joyful mood.

Though movement work such as dance and exercise are dynamic ways of shifting moods, in *Peace is Every Step*, author and Nobel peace prize nominee, Thich Nhat Hanh, discusses the profoundly mood altering properties of the more subtle movement of a smile. He writes:

> *Mona Lisa's smile is light, just a hint of a smile. Yet even a smile like that is enough to relax all the muscles in our face, to banish all worries and fatigue. A tiny bud of a smile on our lips nourishes awareness and calms us miraculously. It returns to us the peace we thought we had lost.* [5]

---

[5] Thich Nhat Hanh, Peace is Every Step (New York: Bantam Books, 1991)

Sometimes when I am experiencing sadness and despair, I remember to take time to smile softly yet intentionally and hold the smile for a number of seconds. When I have done this, I have experienced the miracle of calmness and tranquillity that Hanh describes above.

Just recently I became very irritated at the airline on which I was traveling. Mechanical difficulties and a flight cancellation had prevented me (or so I told myself) from keeping a very important appointment that I had made with a friend. The longer I sat in the terminal waiting for the plane to be repaired the more frustrated I became. Finally when the assistant announced that the flight had been canceled and that the next flight would not be leaving the airport until five hours later, I knew that I had better find a way to shift my mood fast. I remembered the words that I quoted above, and as I inhaled and exhaled slowly (another good way to shift moods) I continued to smile. At first the smile felt very forced, but the more I held the smile, faint as it was, the more peaceful I became. By the time I finally got to my destination and phoned my friend, instead of venting my frustration on my friend, I was able to humorously relay the story to her, and we conversed happily as we arranged for another visit.

Stuart Heller, Ph.D, studies and teaches the psychological changes that occur through movement in the body. I have witnessed him assist others in making positive transformations in self-esteem simply by showing them how to walk with their heads held higher and their shoulders further back. I have also seen a student of his teach a person who possessed arrogant qualities to become more humble and accepting of others by listening and speaking with his chin level, rather than protruding in its typical upward and outward fashion.

As parents, we can make subtle shifts in our movements in order to shift conversations and moods that are not serving us or our children. For example, when we stand towering over our children with our jaws clinched and our hands on our hips, we converse through a space of arrogant self-righteousness. This distances us from our children and puts them either in a mood of defiance or submissiveness. (Neither of which serve parent or child well.) However, if we subtly shift our hands down to our sides or hold our children's hands lovingly as we speak, and we kneel or sit to meet them eye to eye, we create moods of acceptance and respect that in turn allow for genuine, productive, peaceful conversation to transpire.

We will discuss the importance of "body language" in greater detail in a subsequent chapter, but movement, (whether profound like dance and exercise or subtle like breathing and smiling) is an easy, free, and readily available way to shift into moods of peace, ambition, creativity and joy.

Exercise 8

Fill our the following commitment to yourself using at least two of the 6 mood shifters above.

9. _____

On this week of _____, make the following commitment to take care of myself in the following ways.

_____

_____

_____

_____

_____

In closing this chapter, I would like to mention that there have been a score of good books written on the subject of attitude or mood enhancement. The book that had the most profound effect on my own moods and attitude toward my children was another one of Dr. Wayne Dyer's best selling books titled, ***What Do You Really Want for Your Kids***[6]. Bar none, this is the best parenting

---

[6]Wayne Dyer, <u>What Do You Really Want for Your Kids?</u> (New York: William Morrow, 1985)

book I have ever read, and I have read scores of them. He is the parent of eight children, and draws upon his own wealth of knowledge as a parent and his professional experience as a psychologist to assist the reader in setting enlightened, highly evolved parental priorities. His book comes with my highest recommendation.

My intent in these first few chapters, is to have convinced you of the importance of a healthy and positive attitude in rearing children. Learning to create and nourish a healthy parental attitude will set the ground work for successful parenting and will also make the practices in the remaining chapters much more effective.

In the next chapter I will discuss how a parent's use of language and choice of words shapes the self-image of the developing child. By way of my "Johnny and Durk" illustration, it will become apparent how important it is for us to consciously choose the words we use in assessing our children's actions and in building their self-concepts.

Refrigerator Post-it

- A positive attitude about parenting and our children can be learned.

- We can learn to see our children as blessings in our lives and we can hold our careers as parents in a very joyful way by focusing on the many joys and pleasures involved in our day to day interactions with our children rather than focusing on what goes wrong.

Ways to Create a Positive Parenting Mood

- Literally counting and recalling your blessings
- Keeping a watchful eye out for pleasurable experiences that you share with your children or pleasurable moments when you "catch" your children partaking in them.
- Deep relaxation and meditation
- Celebrations on ordinary days
- Having a conversation with a good listener
- Journaling your feelings, moods and experiences
- Listening to music
- Moving your body (exercise, dance, walking etc.)

children are likely to live
up to what you believe of them.

Lady Bird Johnson

Chapter 5

Shaping Children's
Lives through Language

It would be wonderfully ideal if all adults were aware of how influential their choice of words are in shaping the lives of children. If we all possessed this awareness, I am confident that the majority of our words, deeds, gestures, and actions would be positive and would be used to promote our children's self-esteem, creativity and success in life. Unfortunately, there are many loving, caring adults who blindly communicate with their children in ways that promote poor self-image, low self-confidence and even profound deterioration of the human spirit.

One reason individuals do not fully appreciate the power of language is because the impact of language is often so subtle that even the people who are engaged in the conversation are unaware of the power that is generated from their words.

An Example of the Negative Impact of Language

An example of the subtle but potentially powerful impact of language occurred recently while visiting a dear friend. I consider this friend to be a very loving parent, however, during a conversation with her and her ten year old daughter, I heard the mother make a negative comment that if repeated frequently enough, could foster a poor self-image in her daughter.

It occurred when I asked my friend if she might allow her daughter to fly down to visit me in Baton Rouge for the summer. Her reply, though intended as a joke, was actually a powerfully negative message. She said that she would love for me to take her daughter "off of her hands" for part of the summer. Then perhaps she too (the mother) could enjoy her summer vacation without the hassles of carting her daughter from one summer event to another. She then asked me if she could pay me to keep her daughter for the whole summer, or maybe she would ship her to me without a return address.

Though my friend intended the conversation to be humorous, I sensed by the embarrassed expression on her daughter's face and dejected body language that her daughter felt belittled and shamed by her mother's remarks. What I find most sad is that I know that my friend never meant to hurt her daughter. Frankly, I think she spoke in that fashion because society has made it acceptable and fashionable to talk as if our children were nuisances. Though this one particular conversation may not have produced long-term trauma to her daughter's self-esteem, many of these conversations over time could. Chosen unwisely or unconsciously, our words can be one of our children's greatest enemies, especially if those words are repeated often. Chosen carefully, our words can be among our children's greatest allies.

The Positive Impact of Language

Language, is the most powerful tool a parent has in promoting a child's healthy self-esteem. A personal illustration of the influence of healthy languaging occurred when another friend of mine and I were making child care arrangements at our church nursery. This friend has four small children. Their ages are 4, 2 and 1 year-old twins. As you can imagine, having four children this close in age, inspires many assessments and comments by other individuals. Perhaps in response to many of the more negative remarks she has received, the following situation transpired:

Another mother, seeming somewhat frazzled, entered the child care area with her own child. Upon seeing my friend coordinating sitting arrangements for all four of her children, the woman remarked, "Wow, you must have your hands full." Without a second's delay, my friend smiled earnestly and replied: "Yes, they are quite a handful. My hands are filled with happy, loving, little gifts from God, and I thoroughly enjoy each of them!"

After savoring that precious confirmation of the joy of parenthood, I looked to the beaming faces of her children. They were radiating with unmistakable pride that seemed to say, "We know that we are loved, appreciated and a joy to our mother and the world around us."

As I have stated in the previous chapters, in order to become a positive influence in a child's life, and in order to make positive conversations a permanent way of living, we must first experience children as the joy and miracle that our creator has meant them to be. Through the combined experience of joyfulness and awareness, the art of positive communication will be made easy, and once positive communication becomes a routine part of life, our lives will become increasingly more joyful. This is a gloriously progressive cycle that can strengthen and build loving, healthy relationships with all the wonderful children and adults in one's journey through life.

Children Are Like Computers and We Are Like Programmers

As far back as I can remember, I have had a deep desire to understand the HOW'S and WHY'S of life. When I began to explore the premise that a parent's choice of words had a profound and lasting effect on virtually every domain of a child's existence, it was natural for me to ask how and why that was so.

Perhaps the best explanation that I received came from a friend and mentor, Ed Martin, who is a Clinical Hypnotherapist in the city of Houston and an expert at computers. He likens the child's brain to the hardware of a computer, the parent as the computer programmer and the child's inner conversations and beliefs as the software created by the programming.

Essentially, the child's brain, much like computer hardware, is composed of a multitude of cells designed to receive, analyze and assimilate information, and like the computer hardware, it needs programmed software to make it functional in certain areas. We might say, for example, that in the formative years of a child's life, the child's software program of "**Self and world concepts**," is primarily designed by the parents.

As I visualize it, parents, through the use of language, help design a child's computer software with information that will assist the child in developing his beliefs about himself, his beliefs about the world and the subsequent actions he takes as a result of these beliefs. If the programmer and programming are positive in nature - *You are wonderful, you are loved, you are competent, you are cherished.....* the child will internalize these thoughts and will incorporate them into his self-concepts and actions. Theoretically, the information that the parent programmed into his mind will be saved and labeled: *Self-concepts.* If the programmer or programming is negative in nature - *You are stupid, you are lazy and clumsy, you are sickly, you are unlovable, you are a pain in my rear,* then the negative information will be saved and labeled, *Self-concepts* as well.

Later, when the developing child or grown adult must draw upon his present knowledge of self to make a personal decision, he pulls up the *Self-Concept* file. He analyses the data, makes decisions and takes actions based on the information available. By way of the examples below, I will illustrate how parental programming might function in a developing child's life.

Johnny is a typical two-year-old in every way. As any two-year-old does, he trips, he spills and he breaks things. One might even say that clumsiness is a pervasive characteristic of this stage in a child's development - Especially when we compare them to four-year-olds, eight-year-olds, sixteen-year-olds or adults. Johnny's mother, however, through past conditioning and perhaps through a lack of observation of other children Johnny's age, perceives her son as exceptionally clumsy. What's more, in order to reinforce her belief that Johnny is clumsy, his mother unknowingly continues to gather evidence in support of his clumsiness. So, when Johnny does any of the normal two-year-old things mentioned above, Johnny's actions are met with his mother's disapproval and another confirmation that he is indeed clumsy. Johnny's mother's conversation about his coordination (or lack of coordination) are predominantly negative in nature. They sound somewhat as follows:

Messages From Johnny's Mother

Johnny's Mother to Johnny: *Johnny you are so clumsy.*

Johnny's Mother to Father: *Johnny is such an awkward kid.*

Johnny's Mother to Friend: *Johnny has two left feet.*

Johnny's Mother to Johnny again: *You are so accident prone.*

Johnny hears and internalizes his mother's conversations and often overhears conversations that she speaks to others about him. Since mother always knows best, he eventually comes to accept these suggestions as fact. Johnny then begins to focus on the actions that he considers to be particularly clumsy and eventually gathers enough evidence to support his mother's assessment that he is indeed a very clumsy person. If this has been a main theme in his family life, Johnny's primary description of himself might be that of a clumsy, awkward person.

Fourteen years later, Johnny has grown to be a tall, attractive young man. Johnny however, does not perceive himself as such. He is busy obsessing about his clumsiness. We all know a "Johnny". He is the handsome fellow at the high school dance who is awkwardly standing hunch-backed, head held low, in the corner of the room longing for the confidence to ask a girl to dance. Sadly though, every time Johnny thinks he might get up the courage to ask a girl to dance, his *Self-Concept* program spontaneously appears and flashes the suggestion **CLUMSY**. Throughout the years, Johnny has followed his mother's example and continued to gather entries to support the claim that he is clumsy. His self-concepts file is rich with evidence that he is a clumsy person.

Unless Johnny's self-concepts file is updated and reprogrammed through some form of intervention, such as therapy, a self-help book or psychological coaching, Johnny will continue to gather more evidence to support the claim that he is clumsy. In addition, he will likely grow up to feel and act like a clumsy adult. Because his clumsy self-concept is such a prevalent theme, other people may perceive him as clumsy too.

Though this story is hypothetical, there are many real people like Johnny who never achieve their full potential in life, because they have been unintentionally programmed in one way or another to fail. Without the proper programming, they have little chance of discovering the poised and confident self that longs to be expressed.

Let me now take the antithesis of Johnny's story. This is Durk's story. Durk is another typical two-year-old. Durk trips, spills and breaks things. Durk often displays typically two-year-old clumsiness. Because Durk's mother is aware that clumsiness is a typical two-year-old trait, Durk's mother accepts his clumsiness as a normal part of his development. When Durk drops his cup of milk on the kitchen floor, Durk's mother in a calm, loving manner asserts: "It's all right Durk. Spilling milk is something we all do from time to time, and I see that you're getting better and better at keeping your milk in your cup." What Durk's mother is doing is observing, acknowledging and reinforcing Durk's progress toward becoming a physically coordinated and competent individual. She is wisely gathering evidence to support that he is growing more coordinated with each passing day.

In the example above, Durk is being programmed for self-acceptance and self-confidence. Through his mother's endlessly encouraging words and manner, he grows to believe that he is loved, accepted, competent and coordinated. Fourteen years later, when Durk is asked to lead the high-school football team as quarterback, Durk's *Self-concept* program pulls up the assessments of coordinated, poised, adequate, competent... Durk accepts the position as quarterback, and leads his team to several victorious seasons.

Though Durk is a hypothetical character invented to illustrate a point, I feel confident that a story similar to his has occurred in the lives of many successful individuals. I think it would have been very difficult for Joe Montana to have consistently implemented his classic last minute drive from behind for the winning touchdown, if he had not been programmed for success.

As I have suggested above, it is the positive conversations that we communicate to our children that are the backbone of personal success. Occasional carefully chosen negative suggestions must also be spoken in order to empower a child to make wise choices. For example, suggesting to our children that if they touch fire they will get burned, is probably more effective than suggesting that if they keep their hands off the fire, their hands will remain unharmed.

What I propose is that we temper the helpful negative messages we speak with an abundance of positive and sincerely spoken ones. We can only speak sincerely positive messages if we continue to gather evidence to support our belief that our children are loving, caring, precious and **complete** individuals at all stages in their development. These sincere and well chosen messages will encourage children to feel safe and secure in the world and empower them to feel wanted, needed and above all - **Loved.**

Exercise 9

A. Some of the most profound messages I received from my
    parents were:

_____

_____

_____

_____

_____

_____

_____

_____

B. I speculate that these messages have shaped who I am in the
    following ways:

_____

_____

_____

_____

_____

_____

_____

_____

C. Some of the most profound messages I have given to my
    children are:

_____

_____

_____

_____

_____

_____

_____

_____

D. This is how I already think that these messages have shaped their lives:

_____
_____
_____
_____
_____
_____
_____
_____
_____
_____

Refrigerator Post-it

- The words we choose to describe our children often become our children.

- Children's brains are much like computers and parents are some of the major programmers - What we speak to them goes directly into their minds and tends to show up in their lives.

- Children's *self-concepts* are primarily composed of the conversations that parents and other influential people speak to them as they grow.

- *Self-concepts* shape our thoughts and beliefs and virtually all of the actions we take in our lives.

example: If we are continuously told that we are smart, lovable and competent then we think of ourselves and act in ways that are smart, lovable and competent. If we are told we are dumb, unlovable and incompetent, then we think of ourselves and act in ways that are dumb, unlovable and incompetent.

every good thought you think
is contributing its share
to the ultimate result of your life

Grenville Kleiser

Chapter 6

Becoming an Exceptional Resource in Your Child's Development

In this chapter, I will begin to outline strategies for communicating more effectively and positively with your children. In preparation for this discussion, I want to first consider why it is important for us to simultaneously learn to communicate positively with ourselves. I will do this by providing information, exercises and examples which will make the art of communicating affirmatively to yourself (and ultimately to your children) easy and fun.

As a counselor I know that when we learn to speak to ourselves with love and compassion, we begin to hold ourselves as precious and worthy. Then once we begin to hold ourselves as precious and worthy, we also begin to see everyone else in our lives, especially our children, as more precious and valuable than ever before. Speaking from my own experience, I know that part of my journey toward truly accepting my worth and value as a human being, is to have patience and compassion for myself as a parent. I sense the same is true for most of us.

It has been a difficult challenge for me to learn to be compassionate with myself when I'm not parenting up to the standards I have set for myself. I now realize the importance of having this self-compassion in my parenting as well as in all aspects of our lives. Compassion fosters self-esteem and the emergence of self-esteem enables us to break free of the prison of self-destruction into the freedom of self-actualization. What is the pay off for our children? Our children's chances of becoming self-actualized (or highly functional) are significantly increased when they are reared in a home of compassionate, loving, self-actualized adults.

Self-compassion is an essential ingredient for a fulfilling life and for healthy parenting. It creates a space for us to set reasonable rather than unrealistic standards for ourselves and for those around us. Setting realistic standards allows us not only to succeed, but when we don't succeed as we planned, it allows us to view our setbacks as learning experiences rather than failures. Having compassion for ourselves also sets an example for our children to have compassion for themselves. They see their mistakes as opportunities to grow and to learn and - as a precious part of being human. In other words, when we have compassion for our own mistakes, we generally have compassion for the mistakes of our children. Being accepting of our children's mistakes gives children tremendous room to explore, experience and to grow. They grow up to be curious, ambitious and passionate adults - healthy risk takers.

Another side of compassion is to strive as parents and people to focus on all that we and our children do that is right and kind and loving. Then when we err, blunder or trip our way through a situation or circumstance, we can still feel like competent, kind and loving individuals. In my moments of greatest learning, which often coincide with my greatest "mistakes", I reflect on the words of Rabbi Harold Kushner at the beginning of this chapter (which I will quote again here):

> *When we let ourselves be defined in our own minds by our worse moments instead of our best ones, we learn to think of ourselves as people who never get it right rather than as capable people who make occasional thoroughly human mistakes.* [7]

I choose now to see myself as a capable person who makes many thoroughly human and parental mistakes.

So compassion is also having the ability to observe ourselves in the act of doing things well, and honor ourselves for doing so. In my own life, there are clear and glorious moments when I observe myself doing the exact right thing at the exact right time. When I am present enough to make this observation, I acknowledge myself for a job well done. Honoring myself as a loving, caring

---

[7] Harold S. Kushner. How Good Do We Have to Be (New York: Random House, 1996)

parent not only makes me feel good, but it encourages me to continue my quest for excellence in the domain of parenthood.

If the reverse were true, and I were to berate myself for all the erroneous actions that I take as a parent, I'm clear that I would not want to observe myself in the act of parenting at all. If I lost interest in examining the way I parent, then I would inevitably lose my passion to be the best parent I can be. The same is true for all of us. If we reprimand ourselves for our setbacks during the time when we are striving to establish a new habit or pattern, then there reaches a point when we grow weary of all the self-flagellation and consequently give up the commitment to grow and change. After all, why would anyone want to change their behavioral patterns if they shamed themselves every time they noticed the old, unwanted behavior crop up?

This form of self-punishment is all too easy to avoid if we simply stop trying to change our old patterns. The natural tendency to avoid pain and inner-conflict is exactly why habits are often so difficult to break. We reach a point where it becomes too painful to continue the humiliation of shaming ourselves for our setbacks, and ultimately we end our efforts to break through into new behaviors or thought patterns. This is exactly why negative reinforcement does not work well in helping our children establishing new behavioral patterns either.

Just imagine what possibilities might await us all if we continued to reward the emergence of new and desired behaviors while striving to have compassion for ourselves and our children when we periodically slipped into the habit of old patterns. In my personal and profession experiences, this kinder more respectful way of treating ourselves has proven to work very well in establishing lasting change. It's also the healthiest and most loving way of caring for those we love.

There is no magic in this. When we stop to witness and acknowledge our progress and our healthy behavioral changes, these actions and behaviors are positively reinforced. Positive reinforcement theory states that when anything we do (good or bad) is positively reinforced, the likelihood of it occurring again is increased. (This phenomena occurs, because by natural law, we humans seek pleasurable sensations, and are therefore likely to repeat an action when we believe it will give us pleasure once again.) As it applies to parenting - When we observe and acknowledge the healthy skills that we have already developed, we continue to see the emergence and frequency of new and improved parenting skills grow forth from existing ones.

Many of us parents are very good at giving positive reinforcement to our loved ones, but do not extend the same gestures of love to ourselves. So I want to encourage you to treat yourself with the love and respect your deserve, and acknowledge yourself with an abundance of positive reinforcement for all the good things you do in your career as a parent. It is a wonderful way to remain in a mood of peace and joy, and the fruits of this labor are boundless. Let's start right now.

Exercise 10

List 4 things that make you an awesome parent.

e.g. <u>I love my kids so much I read parenting books!</u>

1. _____

2. _____

3. _____

4. _____

If you want to write more than five then be my guest. Take as much time as you would like to acknowledge yourself for your contributions to your children's lives.

That's a fine start. Now let's proceed to the next phase of designing and reinforcing healthy parenting and healthy child rearing practices. The goal of this discussion and these three processes below is as follows:

- to enable you to become a better observer of how your children move and inspire you
- to enable you to become a better observer of your parenting practices
- to remind you to frequently acknowledge yourself for your good work
- to assist you in learning to compassionately review the practices that may be counter productive to your children's healthy development.

Positive Reinforcement for Parents who Rear Healthy Children

I. First, develop an awareness of the times you are in a mood of joy and gratitude for your children: Begin to observe the times in which you stop to focus on the beauty of your child's smile, the precious way that they say certain things, or the way they proudly present you with a drawing that they labored over in an effort to show you their gratitude for you. If you have had a particularly challenging day, you might cherish the angelic qualities of their faces and bodies when they finally fall asleep that night.
Two of the precious reminders that bring me back to gratitude are the smell of my son Matthew's hair and the neat little feeling of my daughter Claire's nose nestled into the crook of my neck when she wants to cuddle.

What I am asking here is that you become an observer of the observer that you are - Catch yourself standing in gratitude of your children. We often live our lives oblivious to many of the wonderful gifts our children bring to us each day. Like their hugs, smiles, laughter, stories, flowers and art work that they present to us as a way of acknowledging us as parents. When we fail to notice these gifts, they never really exist for us - It's like they didn't happen. The child's efforts have been wasted on us.

When we operate in the reverse and remain in conscious acknowledgment of these precious ways our children express love to us, we continuously create joyfulness, peace and optimism in parenthood and in life.

Often, except for a polite thank you, I never truly stopped to give a heart felt acknowledgment to my children or stand in complete gratitude for them when they gave me what I refer to as "every day gifts." Gifts like their art work, *I Love You* notes, or flowers they picked from the side of the road. I am very thankful today for an experience that created a major shift in my ability to notice, acknowledge and appreciate my children, and I am proud of myself for making that shift.

This profound shift occurred on a day when I volunteered to assist my son's pre-school art class in a project they were creating for their parents. The art project turned out to be very detailed for pre-schoolers and time consuming as well, but the children threw themselves into it with passion and enthusiasm. They painted and dyed beans. They tore, rumpled and glued together crepe paper pieces to make trees. They drew pictures, cut out figures, painted flowers and dipped wooden sticks in green paint. All this labor was cheerfully performed in an effort to create a masterpiece for their parents. When the project was finally finished, I could see the pride of accomplishment on each of their faces. As I looked around the room at their master pieces, I thought to myself, "Won't their parents be proud and honored." I could hardly wait until the parents arrived.

The parents finally arrived, and what I observed was extremely disheartening. With few exceptions, most of the parents gave a quick glance at the art work, murmured a patent "Oh! how nice," and stuffed the art work under their arm or in their children's nap sacks. On one level, I completely understood the parent's responses. Given that they were four year-old artists, the art work didn't really look as though it took them two hours to accomplish it. I'm clear that the parents had no idea how hard their children actually worked.

On another level, after working so diligently with the kids, I was absolutely crushed for the lack of acknowledgment that they received. I watched beaming proud little faces turn to expressionless stares. That afternoon I drove home in tears. I cried for them, I cried for their parents and I cried for myself and my children as well. I was most sad, because I knew had I not volunteered to help with the project, I too would have been among those parents who uttered a vacant "Oh! how nice." I knew that I would have also missed a magnificent opportunity to deeply acknowledge my child for his accomplishment and honor myself as the privileged recipient of such a labor of love. I wondered in sadness, how many past opportunities had been lost forever, to appreciate and cherish such gifts from my children. I cried for lost opportunities.

Since that time, I have expressed much more conscious gratitude for any work of art, flower or note my children present to me - For I know whether it took them one minute or one hour to create, whatever they give me they give me from their hearts as a genuine way of honoring me. They are all gestures that say: "Mom you are very special to me." So, all these little gifts have become truly magnificent ways of re-centering myself or observing myself in the present moment of gratitude for my children, for myself as the bearer of life and simply for life itself.

Through my first hand experience as a parent, I know that in the midst of our hectic or routine day to day existence, it is easy to lose sight of what we cherish about parenthood and about our children. It is, however, important that we learn to stay focused on those things that give us pleasure, for we remove from the forefront all that is trying or challenging, and we put the challenging moments in perspective with the joyful ones.

Exercise 11

(You may want to do the following exercise and the remainder of the exercises in this chapter throughout the course of the week, rather than reflect on past experiences.)

In the last several days, I have acknowledged myself as a parent and celebrated and savored the following moments with my children:

1. _____
2. _____
3. _____
4. _____
5. _____
6. _____
7. _____
8. _____

It is my hope that the story and exercise above will assist you in maintaining an awareness of the joys of parenthood - Joyful experiences that are very readily and easy available to us all - Pleasures that inspire a mood of gratitude and enthusiasm to learn and grow as parents. The desire to learn, grow and prosper will make the second and third processes below, valuable and treasured opportunities to serve our children.

II. **Become aware of the times when you are conversing positively with your children:** Before I begin to explain this process, let me first give you a definition and a few examples of positive conversation. Positive conversation or communication is anything we speak, gesture or do that is empowering, encouraging, acknowledging, honoring or praising to ourselves or to someone else. Positive communication between parent and child usually gives both parent and child a sense of well-being and a sense of belonging or unity. Consciously and unconsciously, parents often use positive communication with their children in an effort to enhance their children's self-esteem, to develop certain character traits, to encourage certain behaviors and to discourage others. I have listed below several ways in which we can communicate positively with our children. These communications simultaneously encourage a child's self-esteem, while positively reinforcing desirable behaviors and personality traits.

Examples of Positive Communication

Direct Positive Verbal Communication: *Arthur, you are a loving, kind and smart child. You can achieve anything you want in life.*

Direct Positive Non-verbal Communication: A loving and approving smile and nod of acknowledgment when your child has done something well.

Indirect or Implied Positive Verbal Communication: *You must be very happy that you made such a good grade in math.* (implication: We are proud of you, but being proud of your own accomplishments is more important.)

Indirect Positive Non-verbal Communication: A genuinely sympathetic and reassuring hug after your child has just mistakenly broke your good vase. (implication: I sense you are frightened, and I want you to know that you are more important to me than that vase.)

Modeled Positive Communication: Seeing you and your spouse kiss and makeup after a strong but respectful confrontation. Implications: (a) It's O.K. to disagree, as long as you continue to act with respect toward the other person. (b) Disagreements are a way of resolving issues and don't mean you hate the other person. c) Respectful disagreements lead to peaceful resolutions.

These examples should assist you in recalling some of the many ways and circumstances in which you have already given positive suggestions to your children. Beginning now, when you observe yourself communicating positively with your children, take the time to stand in acknowledgment of the good work you are doing as a parent. Remember that remaining alert to all the wonderful contributions you make to your children's healthy development empowers you to:

1. remain optimistic and ambitious about parenting
2. positively reinforce your healthy and desirable parenting skills
3. continue to affirm your value as a human being.

Exercise 12

In the last several days, I have observed myself giving my child(ren) the following positive verbal reinforcements:

  acknowledged Matt and Claire for helping in garden
_____
_____
_____

The third process involves the use of negative communication.

III.   Observe the times when you catch yourself unconsciously communicating negatively with your children. As I mentioned earlier, not all negative communication is harmful to our children. A reasonable amount of well constructed negative languaging can be very powerful in shaping behavior. However, in order to discern which messages are harmful and which are helpful, we must learn to closely observe what we say and also learn to observe the effect that what we say has upon our children. So in a sense, it is also positive reinforcement for our newly developing parenting skills to "catch" ourselves in the act of negatively reinforcing our children. When we catch ourselves in the negative mode, we can be proud of the fact that we are being more conscious and observant of what we say to our children. Remember, awareness is a monumental step in the direction of healthy change.

Negative suggestions or conversations can be as subtle as an unintentional frown or can be as profound a gesture as a look of disgust. It can take the shape of a parent's physical withdrawal of affection, or can be a blatantly offensive verbal message such as, "You are a worthless, lazy kid." Below I have provided several example of how negative suggestions or messages might look or sound.

Examples of Negative Communication

Direct Negative Verbal Communication: *David, you are a lazy, good-for-nothing kid and you'll never amount to anything.*

Indirect Negative Verbal Communication: *Susan, why can't you be more like your sister?"* (implication: You are not acceptable to us the way you are.)

Direct Negative Non-verbal Communication: Turning your body away from your child in a gesture of rejection when he reaches out to you with an apologetic hug.

Indirect Negative Non-verbal Communication: Lifting the Sunday paper to your face and saying, "I'm listening", when your child is trying to tell you about his great adventure in the back yard. (implication: Listening to you and your stories are not worth my time. The Sunday news is more interesting and more important.)

Modeled Negative Communication: (a suggestion that the child witnesses) When your child sees you yelling at your spouse and calling him/her names. (Implication: It's O.K. to yell, scream, name call and be disrespectful to someone when I am mad.)

Often we are not aware of the impact of our negative messages until we have said or performed them. We tend to "re-listen" to what we have said only after we observe the effects that our negative messages have upon our children's bodies, facial expressions, posture, moods or subsequent actions and conversations with us. If this is the case, and you gain an awareness of the impact of what you have said only after you have spoken it, the most important thing you can do is resist the urge to get angry with yourself. Instead, have compassion for yourself. Acknowledge yourself for giving parenting your best shot, and again, stand proud that you are becoming an observer of your own actions. Remember that many people go through their whole lives without giving any conscious though or awareness to what they speak to their children. You are developing a much greater awareness than the majority of individuals in the world simply by reading this book. You're doing well. Very well.

Once you have gained an awareness of the negative way in which you are communicating, if appropriate, apologize to anyone concerned, then work on a positive alternative for the next time a similar situation presents itself.

Now if you have gained enough awareness to catch yourself in the act of communicating in a potentially harmful way, **STOP**. You may want to literally and loudly tell yourself to STOP, or you may mentally tell yourself to STOP. This STOP technique was established by preeminent psychologist Dr. Albert Ellis, who I mentioned in a previous chapter, to help his clients eliminate negative self-talk. (Self-talk is that sometimes loud, sometimes small voice in our heads that cheers us on and encourages us or nags and berates us.) This STOP technique has worked quite successfully in my own transition from a negative self-talker to a positive one, and has helped me learn to speak to my children in a more positive way as well. Toward the end of this chapter, I will elaborate on the subject of self-talk and how we can learn to keep it positive.

After you have STOPPED the negative thought or verbalization, take a moment and rephrase it in a positive manner. This applies to actions or gestures as well. Remember to have compassion with yourself. Acknowledge yourself for noticing when your negative talk arises, and give yourself a big pat on the back for taking action to positively reconstruct your conversation. I highly recommend that you also let your children know that you are striving to attain a more positive attitude and manner of relating to them. Solicit their support, because kids love to assist their parents in their efforts to better themselves. It helps them to realize that they are not alone in their struggle to grow and to learn and it makes them feel important and needed.

If you are really having a good day you may even catch your negative thoughts before they ever manifest into words or deeds. (You will find yourself doing more and more of this as time progresses.) This time give yourself a bigger pat on the back. Then design and implement a positive approach for accomplishing what you are working to achieve.

It often takes a little detective work to discover the overall tone of the messages and suggestions that we send to our children. Since suggestion can be so subtle, there are other times that we do not realize that we are giving suggestions at all. If you are wondering whether you will ever become a skilled observer of the suggestions that you give, rest assure that this will become abundantly clear as you progress through this text.

In the subsequent chapters, we shall explore in greater detail the overt (obvious) and covert (subtle) ways in which we converse and communicate. The examples of negative and positive forms of communication that I have mentioned in this section are just a sample of what will be discussed at length throughout this book. It is vital to our children that we learn to communicate with them in a positive and affirmative manner, because the information that we communicate has a profound and lasting influence upon how they feel about themselves, how they feel about and respond to the world around them and how much courage and ambition they have in facing the challenges and possibilities that await them.

Exercise 13

In the past several days, I have STOPPED myself from speaking the following negative suggestions, and have replaced them with positive suggestions.

Negative Suggestion	Positive Replacement
e.g. You idiot. Everyone knows the answer to that question.	Honey, you're a smart girl. You can do better in math than that test score implies.

Positive Reinforcement for Developing a Healthier Relationship With Yourself

Equally as important as the three processes above is establishing the habit of monitoring your own self-talk or conversations you have with yourself outside of the domain of parenting. The goal is to learn to be a positive, encouraging, loving influence (parent) in your own life. In turn you will become an even more affirming parent for your children. You can start by asking yourself the following questions:

1. Do you currently call yourself by negative names like stupid or idiot? Yes___ No___

2. Do you presently focus mostly on you flaws or the things you did not accomplish rather than your accomplishments and your attributes? Yes___ No___

3. Does your self-talk also include negatives like "I was never good at math?" Yes___ No___

If you answer yes to any of the above questions, you will likely benefit from using the three step process below as a way to improve the way you communicate with and take care of yourself.

As I mentioned earlier, developing a good relationship with yourself is one of the most important things you can do for the children in your life. It is important, because we must respect ourselves before we can truly extend respect to our children. Secondly, our children learn to respect themselves by watching how well their parents respect themselves and each other.

Exercise 14

Begin this process by developing an awareness of all the wonderful qualities that you possess and of all the accomplishments that you have achieved.

Step I

Directions:

1. Find a sheet of fresh writing paper, then draw a line down the middle of that sheet of paper. On the left, list the characteristics about yourself that you dislike. On the right side, list all the characteristics about yourself that you admire. **(When I do this exercise in groups, some individuals can't think of qualities about themselves that they like. When this occurs, I recommend that they do one or both of the following a) consult a friend who you trust to be honest but loving and b) think of the qualities you admire in others and reflect upon whether you possess these qualities as well.)**

2. Compare the two sides.

3. Tear up and throw away the list from the left side (the side with the criticisms - Most of you have these memorized anyway.)

4. Now keep the side with the attributes handy so that you can continue to make additional observations and refer to the list when you need an emotional lift.

When I first began to compose my own list of attributes, I kept a list in my night stand drawer, in my office and one in my purse. I noticed that I began to have fun gathering evidence in support of all the things I did well. I still do, and my self-esteem and self-confidence grow stronger and stronger with the passage of time. Back then, I referred to my list almost every time I dipped a bit low on the self-esteem barometer. I actually kept the list around for quite awhile, and because I referred to it so frequently, it is now embedded in the deeper consciousness of my mind for quick reference. I now have a strong sense of my accomplishments and achievements as a parent, friend, employee, sibling, daughter and fellow human being, but I still make new additions to my mental list on a regular basis. Honoring and acknowledging myself for who I am, is an easy, handy and effective way to bolster and maintain my ever developing sense-of-self.

If you are like most people, you will be surprised at how many wonderful qualities that you actually possess and how much in life you have accomplished. You may have simply forgotten about all these things in the midst of focusing on the negatives for so long. (This may have been a pattern established in your early life by those individuals who were influential in your development.) If you do tend to focus more on your liabilities rather than your attributes and strengths, then I recommend the following:

- Gather the support of loving, encouraging people and request that they provide you with genuine, well-grounded feedback and acknowledgments about yourself. People who are positive, optimistic and ambitious in nature.

- To whatever extent possible, avoid individuals who are a detriment to your self-esteem - Individuals who criticize and speak disrespectfully to you. Avoid those who try to make you wrong in order to be right and who are angry, resentful, pessimistic, critical and resigned.

- If you feel it beneficial, seek counsel with a qualified mental health professional.

- Read self-help books that are recommended by people whom you assess as joyful and peaceful.

Step II. **Develop an awareness of how often you give positive suggestions to yourself, and affirm that you will continue to give yourself positive suggestions progressively more each day.**

The more you acknowledge and appreciate yourself for who you are, the more you will develop the self-esteem and self-respect needed to live a joyful and fulfilling life. The more joyful and fulfilled you are, the more joyful and self-fulfilled your children will become in life.

If speaking lovingly to yourself is difficult, you may want to follow the morning ritual I have prescribed to friends and clients who requested assistance in developing self-acknowledgment.

Exercise 15

Directions:

1. Upon awakening, stand in front of the mirror.

2. Look yourself deeply into the eyes.

3. In a very loving and respectful way, talk to yourself as if you were your very best friend - a friend who you love, cherish, and adore very much.

(You can accomplish this exercise by speaking acknowledgments, sincere compliments, words of encouragement, an *I love you just for who you are,* and if you have a spiritual nature, by expressing gratitude to the Creator for giving you life.)

At first, many individuals claim that this process is very uncomfortable for them to do. But in time, they report that acknowledging themselves and speaking to themselves as a best friend has a profound and lasting affect on their self-image and self-esteem. This has certainly been true in my own experience. Once I truly realized that I was going to be hanging around myself for my whole life, I decided it was in my best interest to start liking myself. Eventually I became bold enough to declare myself my best friend, and began to treat myself as one. Once I did, my self-esteem made a dramatic improvement and my life became more joyful and peaceful. Essentially, my love and commitment to myself began with the simple action of beginning to speak to myself in a loving and kind way.

Step III. Developing a compassionate awareness of the times in which you are giving yourself negative suggestions.

When you catch yourself in the act of speaking negatively to yourself or saying anything to yourself in a disrespectful way, **STOP** the negative thoughts in their tracks. After you have STOPPED the negative conversation that you are having with yourself, rephrase your concern in a positive way. Example: *I'll go crazy if I lose this job* can be positively rephrased: *If I lose this job, I may be sad and frightened for a time, but I am a competent human being and will surely find another.* If you are having difficulty stopping your negative self-talk, draw upon your list of attributes. Reviewing your list will help quiet your mind enough for you to shift into a more positive conversation where you draw upon your strengths and your loving qualities.

As I stated earlier, there are also many good resources upon which you can draw in an effort to develop a healthy relationship with yourself. Depending on your personal history and current circumstances, a good friend or self-help book may suffice, or you may benefit better from professional counseling.

Working toward excellence in parenting ourselves and our children has tremendous benefits. When we learn to shift our way of thinking (or talking to ourselves) into a more positive dimension, we also learn to shift our way of speaking to others and we shift our way of "being" in the world around us - Our attitude becomes positive, enthusiastic and peaceful. When these positive shifts occur, our children simultaneously shift with us. Both parent and child develop the space to grow into healthy, happy and self-actualized individuals.

Exercise 16

Outside the domain of parenting, in the last several days I have observed myself giving myself the following negative suggestions. I have replaced them with the positive suggestions to the right:

Negative Suggestion	Positive Suggestion

In closing, I would like to share an experience in my personal life that assisted me in developing a stronger self-image. This experience occurred while I was writing this book and transpired as follows:

During the initial draft of this book, I often felt guilty about how absorbed I became in the process of creating it. There were times when I felt like a hypocrite, writing about how to enjoy children when I was neglecting my own in favor of my work. On one particular night, I became really guilt-ridden after choosing to stay home to work on my book while my family went on a camping trip to the lake.

Even though writing my book was a pleasure and a luxury that I seldom afforded myself during my waking hours as a mother of two young children, I still felt very selfish for doin ; so on this particular weekend. As the first evening progressed, I began to notice that my guilt driven inner-battle was preventing me from productively working on my manuscript. I then made a conscious choice to indulge myself in the guilty soup that I had concocted. Before long I became sick of my own mental flogging and got firm with myself. I quieted my unproductive thoughts by implemented the **STOP** technique that I wrote about in this chapter.

After I had successfully stopped the self-defeating conversation, I began to explore my feelings in a more productive manner. I accomplished this by reviewing the last week of my life. I began to remember all of the non-selfish things I had done for my family. Surprisingly, I had managed that week to do many things for my children that were above and beyond the normal scope of my parental duties.

I had spent an hour on one of those nights rocking on the front porch with my daughter and later helped my son repair his Lego® electric train. On another night, I sang my daughter to sleep after reading her much more than her usual allotment of bedtime stories, and had made a special trip to the department store with my son to buy him new art supplies. Much to my surprise, there were many other thoughtful and loving things that I had done that week for my family, yet I was still shaming myself for taking care of my own needs.

Once I had reviewed my week from this more objective perspective, I began to feel good about staying home to work on my book. My mood shifted from guilt to peaceful ambition. I felt much better about myself as a mother and was able to spend the rest of my weekend enjoying my work and the time alone.

Whenever you have feelings of self-doubt or whenever it appears that others are trying to undermine your self-confidence, (as misdirected individuals so often try to do) I highly recommend that you spend some time refuting these assessments in a fashion similar to the example above. You may also want to solicit the opinions of other individuals who you feel are well-grounded and genuinely concerned about your well-being.

All too often criticism is an assessment based on a very small sample of who we are, yet we tend to take these criticisms as global absolutes. For example, someone tells us that we are selfish, and although we may only be acting selfishly in this one situation, or the person who has judged us is not really competent to assess our actions, we still begin to see ourselves as totally selfish in all situations. *He's right, I am selfish and here's the evidence.*

I encourage you to take some time and reflect upon assessments that others have made about you, assessments that you may have begun to believe - Assessments that may only be based on an isolated incident. And while you're at it, you might also consider re-examining the negative assessments that you have made about yourself - Assessments that may have little or no basis in fact whatsoever. Look carefully for the grounding or validity of assessments that may have been made by you or others in haste, anger or as a result of limited information or poor judgment.

In attempting to ground your own, or other people's assessments about you, asking yourself the following questions may be helpful:

- What evidence (facts not opinions) does this person have to ground this assessment?
- How often and in which domains of living (work, family, leisure etc.) is this assessment valid?
- Is the person making the assessment qualified to make it?

Let's look at these questions more closely. If your neighbor tells you that you are a cheapskate, a powerful thing to do would be to ask this neighbor to ground that assessment by explaining to you the actions that you take that make you show up cheap or stingy to her. You may also ask this neighbor under what circumstances and how often has he or she witnessed you acting like a cheapskate. Lastly, you may want to carefully assess the competency of the person who is making the assessment.

When I say assess the competency of the person making the assessment, I would, for example, give a lot less weight to my six-year-old neighbor who calls me a cheapskate because I wouldn't buy a dozen **more** raffle tickets from him, than I would an adult neighbor who assessments me as a cheapskate because I have never bought her lunch (even though she frequently buys lunch for me.)

If I feel particularly distressed by an assessment that someone has made about me, I often reflect upon the pearls of wisdom that were spoken to me by one of my instructors during a course in self-evaluation. She said: *Healthy individuals give weight to the assessments of people whom they hold competent to make the assessment. Neurotic individuals give weight to the assessments of anyone!*

If I held that the adult neighbor was competent in making a well-grounded assessment about me, I might then ask her if there were other circumstances or events that assisted her in making that assessment. I might also ask the opinion of another well-grounded friend and family member if they too can provide evidence of my cheapness. If I felt their concerns had merit, I would then investigate other domains and situations that this character trait may be causing breakdowns in my life and in the lives of those around me. [The neighbor's grounding for the cheapskate assessment was in the domain of friendship and in the circumstance of dining.]

Not every negative assessment that someone makes about us is worth this time and energy, but it is prudent and it is healthy to listen cautiously to and carefully examine those negative assessments that affect or trigger us. I believe that constructive feedback is extremely helpful in our relationships and in our personal growth. What I propose is that you keep it all in perspective. Or as my young son says - Give it a "reality check." There can be real growth and learning from criticism or negative feed-back, but only in as much as we learn to grow stronger and more self-confident.

Our children also benefit tremendously from our ability to ground assessments about ourselves and the world around us. They benefit because we teach them through our example and through our own well-grounded assessments about them, to ground the assessments others make about them, and to ground the assessments that they make about others. (e.g. *Tim, you often share very well, but today you acted selfishly when you took that toy away from Billy.)*

In summary, it is important to remember that the human experience is far too complicated to get "it" right all of the time or even most of the time. The best most of us can do is get some of it right some of the time. So we humans can only create a healthy, balanced and peaceful life for ourselves by balancing the attention we grant to the many areas of our lives that need improvement with the areas in our lives that we have already gained competency and perhaps even mastery!

Exercise 17

Considering that being a human being is a really challenging job, I hold myself as competent and effective and am proud of my performance in the following areas:

1.
_____

2.
_____

3.
_____

4.
_____

5.
_____

6.
_____

7.
_____

8.
_____

9.
_____

10.
_____

Refrigerator Post-it

1. Compassion for our mistakes and human frailties breeds success, health and self-esteem.

2. Compassion for our children's mistakes and human frailties breeds success, health and self-esteem in them.

3. We learn best when we see our mistakes as opportunities to learn rather than as failures. "F" is for feedback - not "failure."

4. Remember to catch yourself in the act of doing things well - especially parenting.

5. Remember to catch your children and other people you care about doing things well too!

6. Speak your requests in a clear, open, honest way. State clear conditions of satisfaction. e.g. (To a 5 year old who is just learning how to feed her dog.) "Emma, Before you sit to watch this TV show, please feed the dog 2 cups of the dry dog food in his silver bowl and empty the dirty water outside on the grass and put fresh water from the hose in his blue bowl." Stated this way, the request leaves much less room for misinterpretations or disappointment. The conditions of satisfaction for feeding the dog should be very clear to Emma.

7. Avoid making requests of your children and loved ones that are hidden, manipulative, "round about," unclear or expected but not spoken. e.g. "Emma the dog is barking, go see if he's hungry." or "Emma, go take care of your dog."

8. The STOP technique is an excellent way of training ourselves to eliminate negative ways of speaking our requests and conversations.

9. Remember to count your blessings at night and throughout the day.

10. When people make assessments about you, remember to ask the following questions.

    A. What evidence (facts not opinions) does this person have to ground this assessment?

    B. How often and in which domains of living (work, family, leisure, friendship etc.) is this assessment valid?

    C. Is the person making the assessment qualified to make it?

11. Remember to acknowledge yourself for all your positive qualities - Particularly on days when you feel you are not living up to the **reasonable** standards you've set for yourself.

I believe the children are our future
Teach them well and let them lead the way.
Show them all the beauty they possess inside.
Give them a sense of pride, to make it easier.
Let the children's laughter, remind us how it used to be.

Whitney Houston - "The Greatest love of all"

Chapter 7

How Language Shapes
Our Lives

In the previous chapters, I have provided examples of how the spoken word or inner voice can affect our own and our children's self-image. In this chapter, I will elaborate on this concept. In specific, I will focus on several domains in the child's life that are most affected by language. It is my belief that by examining the effect of the spoken word, we can fully realize how important it is to be deliberate and conscious when communicating with our children.

Keep in mind that language, whether by word, deed, action or gesture influences almost every aspect of our existence from the way we breath to the way we love, from the way we dress to the way we speak. The communication of language teaches us how to be a child and it shapes us into the adults we become. Religious institutions as well as nuclear bombs are all invented in language before they are ever erected into physical form. This means that we human beings have the awesome power to create our inner and our outer world through our thoughts, speech and then through our actions.

I would first like to state that the information that I provide below is not only applicable to parents, but is designed for any adult who has the opportunity to guide another individual on part of his journey through life. This list includes teachers, counselors, coaches, employers, ministers, den leaders, day care providers, and any person who has the ability to affect another individual's life through language.

Let us now proceed to explore how language can influence who we become and what we create in several domains of our lives.

Self-Esteem / Self-Confidence

Perhaps no other area of a person's existence is more highly influenced by communication than that person's concepts of self. His self-esteem, his self-confidence, his self-respect, his self-image and his ego strength are all developed by input he receives from the world around him. As you can see from the diagram below, self-image is at the core or center of many vital aspects of the self. We need a healthy self-image to achieve our personal best in any of these areas.

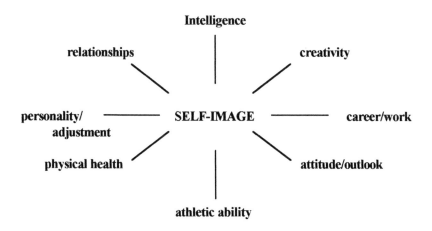

To a great degree, a child's self-image and all of its' many facets (as indicated above) is made or broken by his caregivers way of verbally and non-verbally communicating with him. Carl Covitz writes in *Emotional Child Abuse:*

> *A child facing the difficult challenges of growing up needs a number of things from his parents; their backing and support, their love and encouragement, a sense of stability in the family bond, affectionate exchanges with family members, positive role models, and a sense that his parents love life. A child needs to be liked as a person, and as a unique individual.[8]*

---

[8]Carl Covitz, Emotional child Abuse (Boston: Sego Press, 1991), p. 10.

Likewise, Frank Taylor in his book, *The Pleasure of Their Company*[9] advises that; *listening to children, reflecting back their thoughts, appropriate expression of feelings, respect for the child and helpful praise all help to establish a child's level of self-esteem.*

All of the elements that the two authors list above are available to our children in the verbal, non-verbal and exemplary (modeled) language we speak to them. Positive exchanges between parent and child are fundamental to a child's developing self-esteem, and healthy development. If you closed this book right now, but committed first to provide your child from this day forward with an abundance of genuinely felt positive suggestions that are spoken from a mood of gratitude and peace, then I can almost guarantee that your child will blossom in most, if not all of the areas in the aforementioned diagram.

When healthy self-esteem is consistently being nourished in a child, then the remaining characteristics of his existence tend to fall into place. Healthy self-esteem makes it possible for individuals to overcome monumental obstacles, helps them persevere and find creative solutions when faced with difficult challenges. It helps inspire and motivate them to achieve anything in life that they consider an important and worthwhile undertaking. For example:

What makes an Olympic athlete transcend the boundaries of normal physical ability? Self-confidence does - That inner-voice that says: "I know I can go where no one has gone before." Or what inspires one individual to design a joyful, healthy, well-balanced lifestyle for himself while another may succumb to the numbing properties of over-working, excessive eating or sex or illegal drugs and alcohol additions? I contend that a high level of self-esteem does - for self-esteem creates a space for us to live in

---

[9]Frank Taylor, The Pleasure of Their Company (Radnor: Chilton, 1981) p. 151

passionate alertness (rather than numbness) to all that life has to offer us.

What makes one person learn and grow from his mistakes, while another becomes immobilized by the shame and guilt of human error? Characteristically, it is his level of self-acceptance. People who love and accept themselves, embrace their strengths as well as their human frailties. This gives them the power to use their strengths to turn their misjudgments and errors into opportunities to develop themselves further.

Lastly, what makes world leaders such as Martin Luther King, Mother Teresa and Mahatma Gandhi Noble Peace Prize winners, while others like Saddam Hussein and Adolph Hitler become assassins of their own people? Their levels of self-respect do, for an individual with a high level of self-respect, (not to be mistaken with self-importance) automatically respects and cherishes others and never feels so threatened by another individual's behaviors and beliefs that the other individual must be annihilated.

These are just a few examples of how our self-concepts can affect the other areas of our lives and profoundly shape the world around us. Self-esteem must be continuously nourished throughout our lifetimes. That is why it is so important to continue to align ourselves with people who are loving, encouraging and supportive of our growth. I also believe that as long as we are alive, our self-concepts continue to evolve. Even if the qualities of peace, joy and enthusiasm have been missing from your life for a long time, it is never too late to develop a level of self-esteem and self-confidence that will empower you to develop them. No matter what your personal history, and which mistakes you've made in the past, you and your children are worthy of a joyful life, and there are many individuals and resources out there ready, willing and able to assist you in pursuit of peace and joy.

Developing a level of self-acceptance that promotes fully functional living is a commitment to our birthright and is the essence of what it is to be fully alive. I once read a testament to us all, that I feel best describes the true nature of our existence. It simply but powerfully affirms:

I am worthy (valuable) simply because I exist!

If you suffer from a lack of self-esteem, I encourage you to affirm this phrase to yourself many times a day until you <u>know</u> or "own" that you are truly worthy, simply because you exist. Or perhaps you could remember what a very wise friend once told me, "Each of God's children is his favorite."

I would again like to stress here the importance of carefully choosing the conversations you have with those precious individuals who rely on you to help develop their self-esteem. The basic principles of language's influence on self-esteem are quite simple:

- positive, respectful, loving suggestions foster high levels of self-esteem, while
- negative, belittling, hyper-critical suggestions sabotage our efforts to empower children, and ourselves in upwardly mobile directions.

We will be exploring this important concept further in subsequent chapters.

Attitude and Outlook

I have spoken at length about the influence that mood has in shaping language or conversation, and the influence that language and conversation have upon mood.   There is also a positive correlation between our level of self-confidence and our pervasive moods (attitude and outlook.) I know very few, if any individuals, who have a high degree of self-respect and self-confidence who also have a predominantly negative attitude and outlook on life. Essentially all of the individuals I know with a healthy level of self-esteem and self-confidence, are also optimistic, well-adjusted individuals who spread a lot of joy wherever they go. The two go hand in hand.

Sometimes it is difficult to distinguish self-confidence from self-importance. We may mistake an overt gesture of self-praise or what seems to be "over-confidence" with self-love. Throughout the years, however, I've learned that those who perform the showiest acts of self-confidence, boast, brag, and act as though they are more important than others are doing so to convince us and themselves of their own self-worth. As a friend of mine widely put it, "If you don't hold yourself as precious, you have to try to prove your self-importance, and the prisons are filled with self-important people."

As a rule of thumb, if you think that someone is conceited, snobbish or self-important then he is probably suffering from a fundamental lack of feeling valued or precious. On the other hand, a truly confident person has little need to make showy exhibitions of his importance, or put others down to make himself look good. A truly self-confident person with a healthy level of self-respect walks in the world in honor and respect of everything and everyone in it - including himself. In the chapter on non-verbal suggestion, I will further discuss the role of suggestion in the development of our attitudes and outlook on life.

I would like to note here that in the text I use the word "*suggestion*" as a synonym for anything we say or do (any form of languaging or conversation) that has potential power to influence others.

Exercise 18

Make a list of five people in your life who you hold as optimistic, good-natured and who also have (by your standards) a fulfilling life. Next to each person's name, write down what it is that you think you might learn by observing them.

Nancy	how to be peaceful in a hectic situation

Physical Health

In a lecture given by Bernie Siegel, Cornell Medical Graduate, Professor at Yale University, and best selling author of *Love Medicine and Miracles*, he discussed the travesty of physicians giving cancer patients "death" sentences. Dr. Siegel stated that all too frequently when asked by patients how much longer they have to live, doctors, himself once included, will routinely, give them some statistically based estimation. He was often surprised at how accurate physicians could predict a patient's "Time of Departure." However, the experience I will paraphrase below taught him to see why death predictions can be so accurate, and why people in a position of authority, should carefully select the words they speak to others.

As I remember the story, one day while making hospital rounds, Dr. Siegel came to the bed of a dying man who was not expected to live through the night. According to Dr. Siegel, he had become quite fond of this patient and as their visit came to a close, he found himself unable to tell his patient good-bye. Instead, Dr. Siegel told him he would be back to see him in two weeks after he (Dr. Siegel) had returned from vacation. Two weeks passed and upon his return, Dr. Siegel was met with quite a surprise. The patient was still alive. After the visit with his patient, Dr. Siegel left scratching his head, not understanding how this patient survived for two more weeks. However, within hours after Dr. Seigel left, the man promptly died.

This experience helped change Dr. Siegel's practice and forever transform his life. He began to research and explore the power of suggestion. He began to question whether by giving patients estimated times of departure he had actually contributed to their expectation to die at a certain time. He asked himself what might have happened had he suggested to his patients they had two years or two decades, rather than two weeks to live? These questions and more have led to Dr. Siegel's phenomenal career as an internationally known lecturer, best selling author and scholar on the subject of mind/body medicine.

Through research and years of practical experience with his patients, Dr. Siegel concludes that we can create both illness and wellness through our thoughts and through our beliefs. Based on this principle, he founded an extraordinary group called ECaP,[10] (Exceptional Cancer Patients) which is a support group for critically ill people. It is my understanding that this support group had helped many people significantly prolong their lives despite terminal prognosis, and in others it has helped to put highly terminal forms of cancers into complete remission.

Dr. Siegel claims that his ECaP group is successful, because it is a community which fosters love, acceptance, support and emotion healing. It also helps teach individuals how to live and love life today, and it encourages the belief that there is no such thing as false hope. (Even the gentleman gasping his last breath was given enough hope to live two more weeks.) Lastly, and very importantly, the ECaP support group encourages individuals to use their minds to create physical health in their bodies. This is done through daily affirmations, visualizations, guided imagery, love, forgiveness and group support.

---

[10] ECaP, 1302 Chapel St. New Haven, Conn. 06511 (203) 865-8392

The impact of thought, emotion and mood on the physical body is an area that has gained a tremendous amount of attention in the last ten years and continues to gain momentum and interest in the scientific community as well as the general population. Many call this Mind/Body Medicine or Holistic Health. The premise here is that our physical health is interrelated, and perhaps even governed by, our mental health. Many experts now claim that if we stay mentally healthy, we will likely stay physically healthy as well. Volumes have been recently written on this subject, and research continues to indicate that we can change our health, for better or for worse, simply by the way we think.

Candace Pert, Ph.D., Bio-chemist and pioneer in the field of Psycho-neuro-immunology recently wrote:

> *It took us fifteen years of research before we dared make a connection, but we know that neuropeptides [body and mind altering chemicals] are released during different emotional states. The astounding revelation is that these endorphins and other chemicals [neuropeptides] are found not just in the brain, but in the immune system, the endocrine system and throughout the body.*

She further states:

> *These neuropeptides were seen to affect the functioning of the systems of the body, including the immune system. Viruses use the same receptors [as neuropeptides] to enter into a cell. Depending on how much of the natural peptide for the receptor is around, the virus will have an easier or harder time getting into the cell. So our emotional state will affect whether we'll get sick from the same dose of a virus.[11]*

---

[11] Candace Pert, Ph.D., The Center for Molecular and Behavioral Neuroscience, Rutgers University.

In laymen's terms, Dr. Pert and other scientists are theorizing that when we are happy and contented we release more neuropeptides into our system than when we are feeling unhappy or depressed. According to Dr. Pert's hypothesis, these neuropeptides basically safeguard the cells or protect the cells from viral intrusion by blocking the entrance to the cells themselves. The more neuropeptides we have to block the cell's entrance, the better our chances of protecting that cell against viral attack.

In essence, our neuropeptides act as guards at the gates of our cells, so the more positive we keep our state of mind, the more neuropeptides we have at those gates and the better our chances of fighting off harmful germs. Much of what we currently know about the mind's ability to keep the body healthy has been written in the last decade. However, as long ago as 1922, Psychologist Charles Baudoin wrote *in Suggestion and Auto-Suggestion:*

> *One reason why we have such poor health is because we have been steeped in poor-health thought from infancy. We have been saturated with the idea that pain, physical suffering, and disease are a part of life; necessary evils which cannot be avoided. Think of what the opposite training would do for the child; If he were taught that health is the everlasting fact and that disease is but the manifestation of the absence of harmony.*[12]

I believe Plato made similar observations in the 3rd century B.C., in *Juvenal: Satire X,* when he wrote: *A sound mind in a sound body.* Though I speculate that philosophers such as Baudoin and Plato did not understand the physiological reasons for the mind's ability to affect the body like Pert and other scientist do today, they were non-the-less astute observers. They knew that our

---

[12]Charles Boudin, Suggestion and Auto Suggestion (New York: Dodd, Mead Publishing, 1922)

health is a more accurate reflection of our state of mind than our state of mind is a reflection of our health.

For the most part, Eastern medicine has never lost sight of this truth, but Western medicine, for a variety of reasons (strength of the pharmaceutical industry, fascination with modern technology, and our society's expectation of a quick remedy for everything), has segregated the mind's functions from the body. In Western medicine we typically treat illnesses which often have psychological origins (such as migraine headaches, insomnia, heart and intestinal diseases and hyper-tension) with pills instead of relaxation training or an earnest exploration of the mental stressors, and life styles that cause such afflictions. Fortunately, the medical community is in the process of a major transformation, and in the next few years we will see tremendous renewal, respect and vigilance throughout the medical community for the mind's ability to hurt and to heal the human body. We will also see a major shift of interest from curative and symptom suppressing medicine to an emphasis on preventative medicine.

In my own practice and educational experiences, I have come to believe that the vast majority of diseases manifest from the thoughts and suggestions we give to ourselves and the suggestions we receive from the world around us. For example: Dr. Ed Martin, a Houston based hypnotherapist who specializes in psychosomatic disease recovery, once told me of a woman who came to him with chronic constipation. It was discovered in their therapeutic sessions that two of her favorite sayings were "No sh_t" and "I'll be damned." Once my friend was able to convince his client that her language could be affecting her body, she began to verbally and mentally affirm positive suggestions to herself. One such suggestion was "I lovingly and effortlessly release all that my body does not need," and consequently her chronic constipation was gone.

Take notice of how you refer to your own health and how you suggest that your health is affected by those around you. Do you use the following phrases to describe your emotional state?

• He's a pain in the back, neck or _ _ _!	yes	no
• He makes me sick to my stomach.	yes	no
• My heart aches for him.	yes	no
• I can't stand this any longer.	yes	no
• He irritates me.	yes	no
• This is too much pressure.	yes	no
• This is eating away at me.	yes	no
• He drives me crazy.	yes	no

When we speak these suggestions to our children, there is a double edged sword. Not only are we giving our bodies suggestions for illness, but we are telling to our children that they make us sick. What if we really do get sick? What a burden that would be for a child to live with - for him to believe that he had the power to make another sick, or perhaps even die.

I recently spoke with a 56-year-old client who, in one of our sessions, discovered that since the age of eight, he had been harboring deep-seated guilt about his mother's mental illness and her admission to a long term mental care facility. For the past forty-seven years he felt responsible for his mother's breakdown, simply because he had been repeatedly told by his mother that he was "Driving her crazy." For forty-seven years he had believed that he possessed the awesomely destructive power of being able to drive people crazy. (All because his mother has suggested he was doing so to her.)

Now I know and you know that an eight-year-old child does not have this kind of power, but an eight-year-old does not know this. He will almost always believe what his parents tell him about himself. That suggestion and subsequent belief of my client had stood in the way of him developing a lasting and healthy relationship with anyone in his life, and we are now just nicking the surface of this damage. Please don't ever underestimate the power of the spoken word.

The way out of the trap of making your children feel responsible for your ill health, or setting them up for a "disease mentality"/ "linguistic virus" (language created disease) is to STOP giving yourself and your children negative health suggestions. Make affirmative, healthy suggestions a part of your every day thoughts and conversations. Refrain from using such phrases as the ones on the previous page.

The next time your child comes in from out of the cold and rain, barefoot and soaked to the skin, resist the urge to say "You're going to catch a death of cold," or "You're going to be sick tomorrow." Strive instead to say something like: Let's go put you in a warm bath and take some time to relax so that your body will stay healthy and strong.

If you feel a sniffle coming on yourself, instead of saying "Oh! I guess I'm catching a cold," try affirming that your body is strong enough to keep you well. If you have a competitive nature like my husband, you might affirm that you are "fighting a cold." I feel confident that the reason he is rarely sick is because of his optimistic nature.

Since 1991 when I healed myself of Chronic Fatigue Syndrome and the onset of connective tissue disease, I have had a particular fascination for the field of mind influenced medicine. I healed my body of these dangerous maladies with a simple regime of affirmations (positive suggestions), meditation, and a strong determination to become well. This empowered me to learn to relax and handle stress in more appropriate ways. Since then, I have met many individuals who through mind/body therapy have cured themselves of life threatening diseases, such as cancer and connective tissue disease.

Several years ago I had the privilege of meeting a lovely woman from Canada named Cathy Holmes, who through prayer and visualization therapy cured herself of an advanced stage of Multiple Sclerosis. This woman who had once lost her ability to walk and even sit up, is now taking dancing lessons - Something she would visualize herself doing each day of her self-recovery. She now enjoys perfect health and travels the world sharing her message of faith, hope and healing.

As a college instructor, I also had the privilege of having as a student, a gentlemen named Keith Clark who three years prior to our meeting had been shot four times in the brain. Shortly after the attack and subsequent surgery to remove the bullets, his family was told that he would never talk, walk or even think again. The most remarkable thing about Mr. Clark is that he no longer has the parts of his brain that perform these functions, yet somehow he thinks, he talks and is even learning to walk again. He and I both believe that he has succeeded in beating all odds and making medical history, because he has a remarkably positive attitude, faith in divine order and a strong determination to live.

We have all heard of individuals who experience remarkable recoveries - People who were able to transcend the physical boundaries of what was "normal," or statistically valid . Famous basketball hero, Magic Johnson is one of them. The week after Easter 1997, front page headlines across the country read "Magic Johnson no longer tests HIV positive!" Amazing to most of us, and few of us stop to think about why miracles like this might occur.

I believe as many scientists, physicians, psychologists and lay people do, that our attitudes and beliefs have a tremendous impact on our state of health. Remarkable attitudes and outlooks yield remarkable results. In my assessment, Magic Johnson (even throughout his illness), remained and still is a remarkably positive, mentally healthy and ambitious man. As Charles Boudoin proposed in the quote at the beginning of this section, what if we began to feed our children only healthy thoughts? What remarkable events might occur then?

I do this constantly with my children. My son and daughter no longer believe the common misconception that they can catch a cold by going out in the cold without a sweater or by going to bed with wet hair. They also believe that their bodies were made to efficiently eliminate any disease that is harmful to them.

Even though it has been scientifically proven that a cold virus can only be transmitted by another individual who is carrying the virus, many well meaning individuals still advise others that cold, wet weather, wet hair and bare feet will make them sick. Why is it that science has proven the cold germ cannot be transmitted from simply being cold, but so many people still seem to catch colds after being out in bad weather? Many individuals who study the mind's effects on the immune system claim that the unconscious mind can has a major influence on our immunologic responses. Therefore, an individual who believes he can catch a cold from wet hair, lowers his defenses against catching a cold germ by unconsciously ordering his immune system to avoid the fight against the next virus that comes its way. Why would anyone want to do this? Because the human unconscious or subconscious prefers to be right than happy - or in this case healthy.

To many of you, this may sound like radical conjecture, but before you dismiss this as absurdity, I encourage you to read any of the number of well-executed studies that have emerged from the fields of bio-chemical and quantum mechanical science. We are finding out more and more each day how powerful our minds and our thoughts actually are in manifesting what occurs in our bodies and in our lives.

We can see how this principle applies to children. How often have we heard the well intended mother or teacher say: "You had better get in out of this awful weather, or you'll catch a cold." These suggestions are often made with such conviction that the unconscious mind of the trusting child automatically processes them. Then begins to work to make the illness occur. The child may allow the body's defenses to lower so that the illness has a better chance of infiltrating the body.

In a quote from the *Journal of Alternative Medicine*, Dr. Joan Borysenko states:

> *The body cannot tell the difference between events that are actual threats to survival and events that are present in thought alone.*
>
> *The implications of this work for human learning are vast, for they strongly suggest that internal and external stimuli (memories, thoughts, emotions, body movements, sounds, smells, tastes, situations, settings) can affect a variety of previously conditioned immune responses.* [13]

There is overwhelming scientific evidence that indicates that we have much more control over our own health than we ever imagined. An interesting question to ponder...why is it that so many widows and widowers catch disease and die shortly after the death of their spouses? Is it coincidence? Or can it be that the will to join their partner allows the subconscious to find an outlet for their own departure?

Deepak Chopra, preeminent endocrinologist and internationally acclaimed expert in the field of mind/body medicine, claims in one of his audio-tapes that the most common day for heart attacks is Monday, and the most common time for heart attacks is 9 a.m. Since other animals show no preference for the day and time of

---

[13] "The Journal of Alternative Medicine," Paryallup, WA: Future '
Publishing, Inc., p. 72.

their heart attacks, one can conclude that the catalyst for these Monday morning heart attacks is thought and language - the thoughts people think or speak on a Monday morning that create the stress level needed for the heart attack to occur.

In my own efforts to help my children prevent illness through language, I have advised them that if they do contract an illness, which can occur when the body is simply overwhelmed, they should take a few moments to ask their immune systems to step up its efforts at fighting the germs. I suggest to them that if they do this several times, their body will get rid of the illness in a fraction of the time that it would otherwise take to recover. I also make sure that it is the last suggestion that I give to them before going to sleep - a time when the subconscious mind is most alert.

I tell my children how powerful they are at ridding themselves of illness and disease, because I believe it myself. Perhaps because of my strong conviction and because they are so trusting of what I suggest to them, they rarely advance from a little sniffle to a full blown cold, and are rarely home from school with an illness. Most importantly, I have often suggested to them that they will remain healthy, capable and strong.

Though fighting a cold is a noble battle, the body's ability to heal itself far exceeds its ability to fight off cold germs - or even cancer. World renowned physician, Dr. Dabney Ewing[14] of Touro Infirmary in New Orleans, Louisiana, has had phenomenal success with healing the skin of second and third degree burn victims to near perfect condition. He does this by inducing a hypnotic state within the first few hours of the burn incident and suggests to the person's subconscious mind that the body will heal without scarring. It works, and he has taken and published before and after pictures of his patients to substantiate his claim.

trovues, <u>Hypnosis: The Healing Power of Suggestion,</u> New Orleans, La.

The point that I desire to make is simple. Be very cautious and deliberate about the health information you put into the minds of your children and yourself. The subconscious, where all of that information goes, is a very powerful force in designing our good health and in designing poor health as well.

The field of mind/body medicine is an area where my passion is evident and there is much more I could speak about. I will however, move on at this time and leave it to the interested reader to explore the wonders of modern medical science - Particularly any of the excellent books, courses, videos, television programs or lectures that address the mind's ability to heal itself and create disease.

Mental Health

Mental health encompasses a variety of characteristics, among them are personality, behavior, attitude, adjustment, emotional stability, and the ability to love and be loved. We can even go into greater detail on each of these and list such characteristics as level of compassion, shyness, assertiveness and emotional responsiveness. The list is very long, but the origin of almost all of these states of being remain the same. Except for certain predispositions which appear to be linked with heredity, the basic foundation of an individual's mental health and personality lies within the conversations that occur throughout his lifetime and most importantly in his youth.

Earlier I illustrated the effect that conversation and suggestion has upon the lives of Durk and Johnny. They became the individuals that parents (or other significant persons) expected and suggested they become. Don Hutson, a nationally known motivational speaker, emphasized this point in a lecture I attended for the Baton Rouge, Louisiana Business Owners Association. He stated:

While heredity and environment are both influences of current behavior, the people with whom we grew up and the behavior they demonstrated, expected or praised have profoundly contributed to how we relate today.

It is primarily through our own actions, our language and our expectations (beliefs) that our children learn to be who they are now and what they become in the future. This little known fact is at the very core of my intention in writing this book.

If you show your children that they are important to you, and if you find time to listen to them, talk to them, share "special time" with them, value their opinions, allow them to participate in making family decisions and grant them at least the same amount of respect you would the President or Pope, then your children will become self-actualized human beings. Your children will grow and prosper in directions that give both of you a strong sense of accomplishment and pride.

On the other hand, if you believe that parenting is a burden, that pre-school and adolescence are a curse, or as I once heard a misguided gentlemen say: "Children are God's way of punishing us for having sex." Wow!.. then your children will feel like unwelcome guests in their own homes. I know that many of us can recall that very same feeling from our own childhood. If this occurs, children will also lack the important tools necessary to develop into happy, healthy self-sufficient individuals. What's more, in order to make a negative impact on a child's sense of self, you don't even have to make any of those statements out loud. Your children will simply know how you really feel about the responsibility of raising them by your manner, by your attitude and by your moods. I will discuss this topic further in a subsequent chapter on non-verbal communication.

Education, Career, Athletics and other Interests

I have integrated all of the above categories, because they all consist of aspects of ourselves that we can become, aspects of our being that we aspire to. Essentially, these characteristics are the outward manifestations of who we are. Education, career, athletics and other interests are all developed and nurtured by our feelings of self-worth and by our perception of our own ability to perform and achieve. Our feelings of self-worth and perceptions of what is possible for us in life come primarily from what we have been told and what has been reinforced by significant adults in our lives.

Certainly there are limitations to one's capabilities. For example, you will rarely see a 5'3" individual playing center for a professional basketball team. Nor will you likely find a deaf individual composing a symphonic masterpiece. Yet we have 5'4", "Spud" Webb and 5'3" Mugsey Bogues who play basketball for the NBA, and Beethoven who composed several masterpieces after becoming deaf at the age of 28. All three of these individuals were able to transcend the limitations of what most thought they could never achieve. One could only speculate about the strong messages they received by the influential people in their lives.

Unlike Spud, Mugsey and Beethoven, we often allow our perceived limitations (such as height, strength, intelligence etc.) to limit our possibilities without realizing the power of positive thinking, through which almost anything is achievable. Limitations of nature can be transcended through the power of the mind. Remember Tom Dempsey, the half-footed field goal kicker for the New Orleans Saints. He still holds the record for the longest successful field goal in NFL history, and he did it with only half a foot! My husband once proposed that perhaps it was his half of foot that made it possible to kick so far. My reply to that was, "All the more power to him. He turned what others held as a disability into a very profitable asset!"

There is a bookmark on my desk that states: *If you can dare to dream it, you can accomplish it,* and there is a quote on my refrigerator that states: ***Think you can, think you can't, either way you're right.*** Both of these quotes provide me with the same inspiration. My limitations and my achievements both begin and end with my own thoughts. Accompanied by God's grace, I accept responsibility for my successes and my limitations now. When we are young, however, our thoughts are heavily influenced by the suggestions provided by those around us - primarily our parents, teachers and other significant adults in our lives.

Albert Einstein once predicted that the average human being uses about ten percent of his mental capability. He believed that he utilized about twelve to fifteen percent of his own. If this statement is true, and many scientists say it is, then that leaves a large area of untapped resources in all of us. What if we began to explore this uncharted ground with our own children? With ourselves? What could our children become if they truly believed, and we did too, that they are limitless? What could you become? Do you dare to dream?

What if we stopped giving suggestions such as, "You can't do that because: You're too young, you're too old, you're too weak, you're too unorganized, you're too stupid, you're too poor," and began to speak suggestions such as: "You can do anything you put your mind to doing," "The sky's the limit," "Your future's in your hands," "Dare to be different."

It is also claimed that ninety five percent of the thoughts we had today were thoughts we had yesterday. What if we all decided to expand our own level of knowledge by one percent each day or decided to learn one new fact per day? Perhaps someday ninety five percent of our thoughts could be ideas that we never dreamed possible yesterday. What might we achieve then? The point to all this "Imagine If" stuff is that imagination is what dreams and later realities are made of. It is through a child's fantasies and imagination that he explores the possibilities that await him. If a parent or teacher encourages his child to dream, then a brilliant light will begin to glow. A light that will later shine bright with opportunity.

To the contrary, if a parent or teacher stifles a child's imagination with his own fears that typically manifest as comments like: "That's just your imagination," "why can't you be like the other kids," "get your head out of the clouds," " that's just kid's stuff," or "that boy is such a dreamer, he'll never amount to anything," then the child will learn to stifle his dreams and consequently, stifle the very essence of who he might become. What he becomes instead, if he is compliant, is often what you think he should become - not what he could become. If the child has a rebellious nature, he may very well become that which you fear most.

As the Walt Disney song *When you Wish Upon A Star* suggests, dreams really do come true. An example: when I was a young girl, I loved to watch the Bob Newhart Show. On the show, Bob Newhart portrayed a psychologist. I loved that show. After the show was finished, I use to pretend that I was a psychologist. I would hold group sessions with my dolls, and lay my Labrador retriever on the ground and ask him to "tell me about his childhood." I never let go of that dream - Perhaps because my mother, bless her heart, never told me that I was weird for having it. Through those fantasies, I was able to create a space for my dreams to become a reality. It took me about twenty five more years to actually turn my fantasy into reality, but at the age of thirty-four, I completed my Ph.D work in counseling psychology, thoroughly enjoy facilitating group sessions, and yes, I now ask humans, instead of dogs, to tell me about their family of origin.

If you can muster the courage to allow your child to indulge in his dreams, (My Claire wants to be a dentist/hairdresser/veterinarian) then you can allow your child the freedom to be, as the Army commercial sings; *All that you can be.* You are giving your child the proper encouragement to excel at anything he desires, whether it is athletics, academics, career or other avocation interests. If you carefully select the suggestions you speak to him, steering clear of such labels as: *pea brain, knuckle head, lazy no-good, loser and stupid* while concentrating on life enhancing phrases such *as clever, witty, gifted, talented, creative and winner,* your child will do great things.

Let us now proceed to the "how to's" of joyful parenting though positive conversation. In the remaining chapters, we will explore the various methods by which we give suggestions to our children. In each category, I will provide examples of both positive and negative conversations and how they effect the children who hear, feel or see them. With these examples, your awareness of the power of suggestion will be enhanced, and hopefully you will be inspired to keep your conversations in the realm of the positive.

Exercise 19

I will create a safe and enriching place for my children to explore their own dreams and desires by giving them the following positive suggestions today:

1. _____
2. _____
3. _____
4. _____
5. _____
6. _____
7. _____
8. _____
9. _____

Exercise 20

The words I have spoken blindly in the past that may be getting in the way of my children's self-esteem, dreams and achievements are:

1. _____
2. _____
3. _____
4. _____
5. _____
6. _____
7. _____
8. _____
9. _____

Refrigerator Post-it

Commitment Statement

As the parent of _____, I commit to eliminate negative suggestions that I notice myself making. I also commit to begin **now** to speak the positive messages that I have listed below and others positive suggestions that will empower my child to grow and thrive in healthy, happy ways.

Signed: _____

Positive Messages
(You may want to allow the children to list a few suggestions as well)

_____

_____

_____

_____

_____

_____

Encouragement, recognition, and love lead to
growth. Fear and punishment lead to helplessness,
anxiety, depression, low self-esteem, loss of will,
poor health, and the development of a false self.
Joan Borysenko, Ph.D

Chapter 8

Motivating Children Through Praise, Attention and Effective Requests

Motivating through Praise or Acknowledgment

Frank Taylor in his book *The Pleasure of your Company* states that: *Helpful praise that is accurate helps the child build a positive self-image.*[15]

I use praise, or acknowledgmnet as I prefer to call it, as my first example of emotional support, because acknowledgment is a highly effective form of positive reinforcement. Acknowledgment not only encourages a child to succeed in specific skills, but it also serves to reinforce his budding self-esteem. Recognition or praise can come in many shapes and forms - from the coo or giggle of an infant to the more eloquent use of the spoken language by poets: *How do I love thee? Let me count the ways.*[16]   Where our children are concerned, we do not need to be literary scholars in order to master the art of healthy acknowledgment, but we must learn to administer our praise with sincerity and to gain a healthy respect for its potency.

It is important that we praise our children's efforts or acknowledge them as lovable individuals only when we are sincere in doing so. I learned this the hard way. One day while lavishing Matthew, then four, with his daily allotment of praise, he spoke; "Mom, I wish you'd only give me compliments when I really deserve them." Out of the mouth of babes. His words, though shocking, helped me to see how meaningless my words of praise were becoming to him. Though my intention was to build his self-esteem, by overdoing it, he began to listen to all of my acknowledgments with suspicion.

Since that day, I strive to compliment and acknowledge my children only when I feel sincere about it and when I assess that it

---

[15]Frank Taylor, The Pleasure of Your Company (Radnor: Chilton, 1981), p. 165.

[16] Elizabeth Barrett Browning, Sonnets From the Portuguese

would be helpful to do so. What I often do in place of some lavish compliment, is to remark with interest about the things they have done. For example: Earlier in my career as parent, when one of my children would show me that they had cleaned their room, I would exclaim with exaggerated enthusiasm how wonderful the room looked and what a marvelous, fantastic, excellent job they had done. What I didn't know at the time was how smart they were at detecting my exaggerated enthusiasm. Now when they proudly announce that they have cleaned their rooms, to show my interest, I accompany them upstairs, and then I carefully look around and favorably remark about how I notice that all the stuffed animals are placed neatly on the shelf and how most of the clothes seem to be put back tidily into the drawers. My enthusiasm is displayed by my interest in walking up to their rooms, and the reinforcement occurs by my simply acknowledging things that I notice have been cleaned. There is no lavish, exaggerated praise that will be heard suspiciously - only the powerful motivator of genuine recognition.

If we praise our children when we sincerely mean it and we remember to do it regularly but not constantly, then our acknowledgments will have a strong and healthy impact upon our children's self-image and the likelihood of them repeating the acknowledged character trait or behavior will increase.

It is also very important to tell our children how wonderful, precious and lovable they are at times when they are simply being themselves and not doing anything particularly impressive or compliant. This teaches them that they do not need to perform or act in any special way to be loved by us. It teaches them that they are loved for who they are - not what they do. This is what is referred to as "unconditional love."

An even more awesome experience for children is to be told they are lovable and precious at times when their actions have been met with disapproval by us. This form of acknowledgment teaches them profoundly unconditional love, and is the most important message we can ever give our children. It teaches them that they can make mistakes (which we will all continuously do throughout our lives) and that their mistakes are just a part of being preciously human. The power of this message cannot be stressed enough. When we don't have permission to make mistakes and still feel loved by our parents, we often grow up to be adults with emotional and spiritual difficulties such as low self-esteem, tremendous fear of making mistakes, anxiety or neurotic disorders, perfectionistic standards or deep resignation and depression.

As I stated above, acknowledgment does not need to come in the form of a literary work of art or in some lavish package of compliments. Provided the recognition comes from a voice of authority (as all parents have), powerful and profound recognition can occur through a simple one syllable word like good, by the gentle touch of a hand, or in the subtlety of an approving grin. Below I want to share a story with you that will illustrate just how potent a sound as simple as a "Ha" can be in reinforcing behavior.

One night while watching a popular late night talk show, the host was asked by one of his guests: "When was it that you knew you had really made it in show business?" In response to this question the host related the following story:

He stated that he really knew he had made it when, Milton Berle, notorious for sitting through other comedians stand up acts with a poker face, came to his stand up routine at a night club in New York. Having Milton Berle in the audience made him very nervous, but as it turns out, he succeeded in telling a joke that made Mr. Berle laugh for a moment out loud. The talk show host claimed that at that very moment he knew that he had made it big as a stand up comic.

Thus even in the simplest forms of verbal encouragement such as laughter, there can be mighty power. It is the awareness of the impact of our words and of our authority and the judicious use of both that allows us to become most effective at being a positive influence in the lives of others. Sincere acknowledgment by others, especially our parents, is necessary to grow healthy and happy. It allows us to see and experience ourselves as a contribution to the world around us, and it is only in the realization that we are a contribution to the world around us that truly healthy self-esteem evolves.

Exercise 21

List two situations when you may have "overpraised" your child's efforts and record what it is that you said that now seems insincere. Do you feel your child may have sense the insincerity?

1. _____

_____

2. _____

_____

List two situations when you may have neglected to acknowledge your child's efforts that could have been important feedback for him to receive. Then reflect on the following questions. How do you think he would have felt if he had been given a sincere acknowledgment at that time? How might he have felt in not getting the acknowledgment?

1. _____

_____

2. _____

_____

List three sincere acknowledgments that you would like to give your child right now that you feel are important for him to hear from you. If you have more than one child, please make a separate list for each. (Remember that your child does not need to do anything in particular to receive acknowledgment. It is very powerful to be acknowledged simply because we are precious and unique human beings or because our mere presence is in some way a contribution to our loved ones.)

e.g. <u>Mary, Dad just wanted to tell you how precious you are to</u>
    <u>me. I'm so glad you're my daughter!</u>

1. _____

   _____

2. _____

   _____

3. _____

   _____

I promise to give these three acknowledgments to my child the very next time I see or hear from him / her. I may also send these in a note card as well.

                              Signed _____

I hope that this exercise has provided you with some insight into the importance of acknowledgments and the effect that receiving them or not receiving them has upon us and our children.

Motivating Through Requests

Let us now examine requests as a way of verbally or linguistically motivating children. I have chosen the following examples to bring to your awareness the different ways in which you can make the same request. I will let you be the judge of which you feel may produce the best results for you and at the same time make your child feel like a winner in life.

Listed below are a variety of ways in which Dad can ask little Timmy to close the door. Dad can give Timmy a:

Direct Request: *Timmy please close the front door right now.*

Indirect Request: *It sure is cold in here with the door opened Timmy.*

Covert/Indirect Request: *I guess I'll just wait for the butler to come shut this door for me..*

Negative Direct Request: *Timmy, close the door or you're going to be punished.*

Negative Indirect Request: *Timmy, don't leave the door open.*

Double Negative Indirect Request: *Timmy, if you don't shut the door, I'm going to kick your _ _ _!*

After reviewing the requests above, which do you think would best support Timmy to remember to keep the door shut? On first thought you might say the double negative, direct suggestion, for it is often spoken with a lot of conviction. Actually, if Timmy feared his father's wrath, then it probably did make Timmy close the door a lot more quickly than a clear and respectful request. However, a more important question is whether it would assist him in establishing a successful pattern of closing the door in the future? Most behavioral scientists who study the effects of both positive and negative reinforcement claim that administering a hostile, negative suggestion may produce immediate results, but because we are not telling Timmy what we do want him to do, "close the door," Timmy is not receiving the proper information to remember what to do in the future.

In other words, when you simply say "Don't leave the door open," a two, three or even four-year old must deduce, "What does it mean not to leave the door open." Since he still does not possess well refined reasoning skills, he may fail to realize that "Don't leave it open," also means to "Keep it closed." This is the greatest distinction between an indirect and a direct request. An indirect request only implies what we want or need " I want you not to leave the door open" - a direct request speaks directly and specifically into our needs and desires. "I need you to close the door immediately." A little confusing? Just think how a three year-old feels. Even older kids will be caught off guard and process the information more slowly if they must first deduce the meaning of the request.

Most behavioral scientists claim that the respectful, positive and direct request, "Timmy please close the door immediately," and a sincere acknowledgment *Thank You* of his favorable response are the most effective ways of helping Timmy to remember to continue to shut the door in the future. Why? Because a) the request is clear, and b) children thrive on acknowledgment and on loving attention.

In other words, before long and with a little bit of consistent positive reinforcement, Timmy will have formed the habit of consistently closing the door. He will do so because:

- He clearly understands the request (The door is to be kept closed.)
- He realizes that his father noticed and is pleased with him for shutting the door.

- Timmy, like all children, searches for ways to get loving attention from Mom and Dad. If he gets the reinforcement that he is seeking, he is likely to repeat the behavior in the future.

In contrast, negative, covert, humiliating, passive-aggressive and sarcastic suggestions are highly ineffective methods of communication because they promote confusion, defensiveness and resistance in anyone receiving them. As any adult knows, it is very unpleasant and embarrassing to have someone bark orders at us in a disrespectful and aggressive tone. We have all had at least one boss, teacher or coach who used anger and bullish authority to manipulate us into getting what they wanted from us, and we also know how resentful we were in being treated this way. Yet many of us still speak to our children with anger and disrespect and expect that our children will want to comply with the request we make of them. Why should they feel any different than we do when we are spoken to in this way? No one, not man, woman or child is eager to comply with requests that are made through the voice of anger and self-righteous expectation.

Always and Never

In the work I have done counseling families, I all too frequently see counterproductive, covert, angry requests being spoken to those who are held most dear. Our session may be percolating along nicely, both husband and wife making headway through the obstacles that have brought them to therapy, when out of the blue comes a request in the form of an "always" or "never" statement. These always and never statements are among the most damaging, ineffective requests one person could make to another. They generally sound somewhat like this:

The husband may say: *One reason our marriage is falling apart is because you NEVER come with me to any of the football games.*

The wife may reply: *That's because you ALWAYS ask your friends to go first. I'm NEVER your first choice, so I figure why bother.*

Both the always and never statements then produce an instantaneous call to defense by both parties. They become so involved in defending themselves, that they cannot even begin to listen to the request being made. (Though trained to do so, it is sometimes difficult for me to recognize the request as well.)

The next remarks may sound much like the following:

The husband: *That's not true! You **never** will commit to come unless you have nothing better to do, and even when you do say you'll come, you **always** cancel when something better comes up. Remember when I asked you to the Buffalo game? You said you'd come, then you changed your mind and went to dinner with Teresa? It was only after you canceled, that I asked Buddy to come later.*

Or the wife may say: *Well, I don't come with you to football games, because you NEVER come with me to the Symphony.*

At worst this litany might continue until one or both parties are sufficiently insulted, or simply tired of the endless argument. If I am given permission, I might encourage them to explore the real issues (or requests) being hidden behind the negative verbiage.

The simple request that both the individuals above are trying to communicate is that they want to feel wanted, needed and important in the other person's life. If they had skipped the accusations they may have been able to communicate those requests in a way that produced mutually satisfying solutions for both. In essence, by placing each other in defensive positions, couples like the hypothetical one above and children as well, often fail to understand our requests. They and we become so involved in defending our positions that we rarely hear the concern behind the words. What if the conversation had gone more like this?

The husband would say: *I would feel much more special to you and be a lot happier in our marriage if you would show interest in what I am involved in - like coming to the football games with me.*

Or the wife might say: *I like to feel important in your life, and you can help me to feel special by giving me the first invitation to come to your football games and by coming to some of the events that are of interest to me - Like the symphony.*

Without the barrage of typical accusations, insults and criticisms, the discussion may very likely transpire into a win/win situation for both individuals above. In applying this to our children, when we make direct positive requests of them, we are much more likely to get them to listen and respond favorably to our request than we when we call them to defense. I know in my own experience as a parent, when I make a firm but respectful request such as; Claire, please remove your shoes from the kitchen right now and put them in your room, I am much more likely to get her to peacefully comply than if I speak it in a manner such as: Claire! You NEVER put anything away. Get these shoes out of the kitchen this instant!

As the old adage suggests, I do catch more flies with honey than I do vinegar. I suspect that you will find the same to be true in your home as well. Speaking to our children with kindness, respect and dignity, however, is not just a tool to be used to gain a desired response from them. The manner in which we speak to them will also set a precedent for the way they allow their own husbands, wives, children, employees and friends to speak to them in the future and will likely be the way they speak to others as well.

Motivating through Attention or Neglect

As I mentioned in the previous section, acknowledgment and recognition are both powerful reinforcers for desirable behaviors. Unfortunately, the same holds true for undesirable behaviors. Whether it is "nice" attention or a reprimand, a parent's attention to a child's undesirable qualities or actions can be a positive reinforcement for those traits to continue. According to the text *Adjustment and Growth*,[17] positive reinforcement (in this case, simply noticing a child's behavior) is the most successful way of increasing a certain behavior. So, what do we do if our child is displaying an annoying behavior, such as jumping on the sofa or whining, despite the fact that in a firm but respectful way we have asked her to quit?

Considering that both of these actions are typically designed to get a parent's attention, we may consider the following: According to same text, the most successful way of eliminating a behavior is to ignore it. This may come as a surprise to many people who believe that punishment is a stronger method for eliminating an undesirable behavior, but punishment may not deter a child who is eager or longing for your attention.

For many centuries we assumed that punishment was the best behavioral shaping tool available. Children were considered unruly and impulsive creatures that must be physically and verbally tamed and molded into civilized human beings. Spare the rod and spoil the child was the motto. Few people understand even today that this quote did not address corporal punishment of children. The Hebrew word translated as "rod" actually spoke of one's authority or mastery, not a physical rod. We can see the symbolic nature of the rod [staff] in the Catholic Church today, as the Pope carries a staff in representation of his authority. Biblical scholars

---

[17] Vince Napoli, Adjustment and Growth (St. Paul: West Publishing, 1985), p. 87-88.

believe that the quote spoke of providing direction and guidance to children so as not to spoil them. It did not endorse or condone beating a child into submissive behavior.

Fortunately, enlightened individuals have discovered that children are born with many more loving and life giving qualities than they are destructive ones. We are also learning that it is not through the punishment of undesirable traits that children thrive best in life. It is through the encouragement and support of their good qualities and strengths that we provide the best environment for a child to grow up confident, happy and an asset to society.

Now I am certainly not proposing that we eliminate punishment from our list of disciplinary options. As a parent and as a professional, I know first hand that respectful, well planned, well-executed revocation of a privilege (grounding) can be a strong motivator for behavioral change. What I am stating is that there are many reasons why punishment should be considered as a later alternative rather than first option in healthy behavioral shaping - Primarily because punishments such as yelling, lecturing, hitting and scolding can actually be positive reinforcements in disguise.

Children crave attention, and if you have had children in your care, you know that they will do just about anything to get it. A pre-school child who is trying to get your attention by teasing his younger sister or a teen who is crying for attention by maiming his body with body piercing from head to toe, will likely continue to do so if it consistently or frequently gets attention that he otherwise does not receive.

Essentially, by focusing your energy on the child's undesirable actions, he is receiving the attention that he needs and craves. It may not be warm, affectionate attention, but as research and observation have sadly affirmed, children will prefer negative attention to no attention at all. Simply put, children will do whatever it takes to be noticed by you. As long as their tactics work in getting your attention they will continue to utilize them!

For example, when I see a child who is constantly acting in highly disruptive or destructive ways, I also see a child who is starved for healthy attention. Often these children are ignored when all is going well, and it is only when they are disruptive that they are given attention. The point of this discussion is that negative attention can be a positive reinforcement if it satisfies the child's need for recognition. Therefore, one of the best ways to eliminate unwanted, destructive or "acting out" behavior is to give the child lots of healthy attention when he is behaving in desirable ways.

I hope that it is becoming evident why we should focus our attention and our acknowledgments on the characteristics and behaviors we want our children to exhibit. It should also become evident why we need to ignore some of the less harmful characteristics and behaviors that we want to extinguish - like when a child comes home with his hair dyed purple and pink for the purpose of having us notice that he's alive.

I suggest we ignore the harmless attention seeking strategies like peculiar colored hair, because they are usually done for attention. However, as a mother, I fully realize that I cannot ignore harmful behaviors, like when my daughter is dragging her cat by the tail, or my son's attempt to parachute off the top of our roof. Though these things may also be done to get my attention, I believe it is important for my children to know that their behaviors are harmful to themselves and to the world around them. These actions must be dealt with as they arise, because they involve the safety and dignity of my children and of others around them.

There are times, and for me times like those above, when for their safety or the safety of others, more punitive measures are in order. If my son has attempted to jump off the roof, I will take his make-shift parachute away and send him to his room pondering the possible consequences of parachute jumping off of the roof. If my daughter has harmed he kitten, I will remove the kitten and my daughter from each other's company. As a rule, if a situation is emotionally or physically detrimental to anyone, attention, perhaps even negative attention, may be the best course of action. The vast majority of other problematic behaviors can often be resolved in one of the following manners:

- By finding the reason for the undesirable behavior *(I sense my son is jumping on the sofa to get my attention.)*
- By preventing reinforcement of the undesirable behavior - Not yelling at him for jumping on the sofa or making a big deal of his misbehavior.
- By taking positive measures to eliminate the reason for the behavior by:
- diverting the child from the unwanted behavior *(Jack you may use your trampoline outside for jumping* - and usher him outside if you need to,)
- promise that within the next several hours you will spend time with him - set a clear time and activity so that the child knows he can count on getting your attention.
- giving him loving attention throughout each day.

Reinforcing Sibling Rivalry

I would like to confess that I have often, more so in the past, reinforced a most prevalent form of undesirable behavior - sibling rivalry - by getting into the middle of my two children's disagreements. However, after reading Adele Faber and Elaine Mazlish's book *Siblings Without Rivalry*[18], I realized that my children were often fighting to get my attention, and better yet to see if I would form an alliance with one of them or the other. My children probably fought, because they knew that as long as they were playing cooperatively, I would proceed with whatever project I was involved in. They also knew that when they were

---

[18] Adele Faber and Elaine Mazlish, Siblings Without Rivalry (New York: Avon Books, 1987)

ready for my attention, all they needed to do was begin to fight or stop cooperating, and that would send me running- my peace and quiet shattered.

Now when I am alert and aware, I frequently reinforce their cooperative play. I will often join them, sometimes only for a short time, when things are going smoothly. I give them lots of praise for cooperative play, and let them know how much I appreciate them. If I cannot spare a few minutes during their playtime, I let them know that because they have played so well together, I will play with them as soon as I am finished with whatever I am doing.

I won't mislead you, noticing good behavior is, at first, not as easy as noticing bad behavior. Disruptive behavior disturbs our peace of mind and interrupts our moment. It is often a rude awakening. With a little time and patience however, the melodic tone of peaceful and constructive behavior will come to the forefront of your awareness. You will then find yourself verbally and non-verbally reinforcing these highly desirable behaviors with more and more frequency. In turn, you will find the frequency of pleasant, appropriate behaviors increasing in your environment as well. It is a wonderful upward spiral that every family, classroom, day care, work or therapy setting can enjoy.

I would like to end this chapter with one last statement. It is my experience that children need attention and acknowledgment as much as they need food and water - so do adults for that matter. We all have a strong desire to be acknowledged and noticed. When we are truly acknowledged for who we are (not what we do), we feel valued, loved and a strong sense of belonging or connection to the world around us. When we are neglected or harshly criticized, the opposite occurs. We feel unworthy, unimportant and disconnected. Please give your children lots and lots of recognition and loving attention. They deserve it, and they truly need it to grow into healthy adults.

In this chapter I focused on praise, affirmative direct requests and attention as ways of encouraging behavior and character traits. In the next chapter, I will delve more deeply into the power of spoken language itself. I will bring forth several distinctions about positive and negative suggestions, and will discuss which types of conversations are most successful in rearing healthy children.

Refrigerator Post-it

- Sincere praise and acknowledgment are two important cornerstones of healthy child development.

- If praise is insincere or overdone, children often know this and will begin to hear our acknowledgments as meaningless or hollow.

- Remember not only to acknowledge age-appropriate and age-competent work, but to acknowledge your child simply for being who he is - precious and valuable to you.

- Always and never statements are ineffective ways of making requests.

- Behaviors will likely continue to exist if we reinforce them with any attention - positive or negative.

- Behaviors will likely diminish and disappear if we do not reinforce them.

- Basically harmless negative behaviors that are used to get parent's attention are best ignored.

- Harmful negative behaviors that are used to get parent's attentions are best dealt with and the source of the problem behavior confronted.

- The very best way to prevent negative attention getting behaviors is by giving our young children loving attention throughout the day and by carving out special time each day to give our older children an opportunity to be in positive, supportive conversation with us as well.

For as a man thinketh in his heart,
so is he.

Proverbs 23:7

Chapter 9

Distinguishing Between Positive and Negative Verbal Suggestions

In the last chapter, we began to examine the difference between negative and positive ways of speaking our requests, concerns and acknowledgments to those we love. In this chapter we will make further distinctions between affirmative, health promoting conversations and conversations that may be detrimental to you and to those influenced by your messages. It is my goal in this chapter to provide you with distinctions that assist you in distinguishing empowering suggestions (conversations) from the negative ones that undermine our children's healthy development. Below I will discuss two concepts that are fundamental to creating a home environment that is enriching and nourishing to the human spirit.

Concept I: There is a positive action to replace every negative action that occurs.

Concept II: There is a positive word to replace every negative word that is spoken.

So that we may conduct a modest test of this hypothesis, I have created the following exercise. This exercise, will assist you in seeing that negatively phrased suggestions can be redesigned into more positive ones. This is a shift of focus from behaviors that we don't want to see, to ones we do want to see. This exercise may also serve to aid you in developing or increasing your awareness of how relatively easy it is to keep the task of parenting on a positive course.

Exercise 22

Instructions: On the space provided under each of the following suggestions, construct a request or statement that turns it into a more positive one.

1. Stop hitting your brother.

   e.g.: <u>Please move away from your brother, and go play in the toy room.</u>

2. I can't stand it when you leave the door open!

   _____
   _____

3. You <u>always</u> lose your mittens!

   _____
   _____

4. <u>Don't forget</u> (double negative suggestion) to do your homework.

   _____
   _____

5. Why can't you be helpful like your sister? (Hint: create a statement that does not compare one   child   to another.)

   _____
   _____

6. When are you going to grow out of this clumsiness?

   _____
   _____

7. You <u>never</u> give me my phone messages!

   _____
   _____

8. Stop whining, because I can't hear what you are saying.

_____

_____

9. Don't touch Aunt Harriet's crystal vase. You might break it.

_____

_____

10. Shame on you, you bad boy. You broke Aunt Harriet's vase.

_____

_____

Note: There are many positive ways in which we can phrase each of these statements above, so there is no one perfectly correct answer. Below in 1.N - 10.N I will reiterate the negative suggestions above and in 1.P - 10.P, I will provide you with a list of the suggestions and statements that I might choose instead. I will also provide a brief explanation of why I would choose a particular manner of speaking over the examples provided above.

SAMPLE ANSWERS AND EXPLANATIONS

1.N *Stop hitting your brother.*

1.P *Please treat your brother's body gently. You may kiss him, and hug him or sit with him on your lap.*

Perhaps Jenny is hitting her brother, because she wants to interact with him but does not know how to appropriately do so? By requesting that Jenny stop hitting her brother, you have not outlined what it is that you would like her to do instead. By asking her and demonstrating to her how to treat her brother's body gently and loving, you are letting her know how you would like her to act. When you describe these gentle acts, you are helping Jenny to form a clear idea of her interactive options with her brother. Remember, when you state what you don't want, but fail to state what you do want, a young child's reasoning skills may not be equipped to deduce the solution. When you stick with suggestions that state the behavior you want to see from the child, there will be little question in the child's mind as to what you expect of her.

2.N *I can't stand it when you leave the door open.*

2.P *I appreciate it VERY much when you close the door.*

The rule above applies here as well. State the behavior that you want. Your desire is to get her into the habit of closing the door.

3.N *Jenny you always lose your mittens.*

3.P (Spoken after Jenny returns home with her mittens) *Thank you for remembering to bring both of your mittens home from school today. I see you are becoming very responsible for your things!*

The statement in 3.N is a classic example of a negative suggestion. By saying "you always lose your mittens," you are setting up Jenny's little computer program to remember to forget her mittens. After all mom is always right, and she has said that Jenny ALWAYS forgets her mittens.

4.N *Don't FORGET to do your homework.*

4.P *Please remember to do your homework.*

Research has suggested that when we tell someone to remember something, the likelihood of them remembering it is greater than when we say: "Don't forget." Can you hear the two negatives above DON'T AND FORGET? It takes the same amount of effort, and has a greater impact on our children when we say "Please remember."

5.N *Why can't you be helpful like your sister?*

5.P *I know that you can be a good helper. I really appreciate it when you pitch in and help the rest of us clean up the house.*

"Why can't you" is a way of suggesting that she can't. You are also asking her to make an excuse for who she is. (Not her sister.) By suggesting that she can be helpful, you are encouraging her to do so. By avoiding unfavorable comparisons, you are affording your child the dignity and honor she deserves as a unique individual.

6.N *When are you going to grow out of this clumsiness?*

6.P *Have you noticed that more and more each day you are becoming steady and sure on your feet. You really are growing up, aren't you?*

In the statement in 6.N above, we are encouraging him to remain clumsy. Again, we are also asking him to make an excuse for his behavior. I wonder if any parent truly expects their child to know the answer to any of the barrage of other "When are you going to..." questions. I once heard a mother ask her son the classic rhetorical question; "When are you going to grow up," and when her son said "Tomorrow Mommy," she slapped him for being disrespectful. As I witnessed this, I did not detect sarcasm in this young child's voice. Quite truthfully, I thought the child was making an honest attempt at assuring his mother that he would try to conquer his "liability" of childhood tomorrow. In the statement in 6.P, we are clearly encouraging him to be steady and poised through our positive reinforcement of these traits.

7.N *Jim, You NEVER give me my phone messages!*

7.P *Jim, I really appreciate it when you give me all of my phone messages, and I am going to leave this paper next to the phone to help you remember to record any and all phone messages in the future. Thank you.*

Like Jenny who ALWAYS loses her mittens in 3.N, Jim NEVER remembers to give her phone messages. With that negative reinforcement, he's probably not going to start remembering any time soon. However, if we give Jim a little help by reminding him of your needs, by giving him a pad and pencil ahead of time, and by periodically thanking him for remembering the phone messages, he will probably remember to take down messages more consistently in the future.

8.N *Stop whining, because I can't hear what you are saying.*

8.P *It sounds like you are upset. If you speak clearly, I will be able to hear you and understand what you need.*

Whining occurs when a child is hungry, tired or frustrated. It can also be a tool used to wear parents down so they will submit to the child's request. At times when your child's request is reasonable and you intend on fulfilling the request anyway, ask the child to speak the request clearly to you, and insist that only then will you consider granting the request. Since the child wants his request honored, this will motivate him to speak clearly, and by your honoring the request, you will positively reinforce the quality of making a request in a clear manner.

Consistency is the key to eliminating whining. If a child, no matter how old, gets what he wants by whining, then he will continue to use whining to get what he wants or needs in the future. When my children were younger, I would say to them: "Use your words clearly, so I can understand you." If they continued to whine, I would then say: "Since you are whining, you now need to wait five minutes before you can ask me for what you want again, and it must be in a polite voice." Both requests are concise and to the point and were quite effective in teaching my children how to make requests in a clear, polite manner.

9.N *Don't touch Aunt Harriet's crystal vase. You might break it.*

9.P *Please leave Aunt Harriet's vase on the shelf. It's very beautiful isn't it. Now you can admire (enjoy) it with your eyes. Your hands must stay at your sides.*

Whether child or adult, there is nothing more tempting to a curious spirit than to have someone say "don't touch." To the more free spirited child, it is an invitation to explore the thrilling sensation of that which is considered taboo. Even if you want to say "Don't touch the vase," it would be better to say, "stay this far from the vase" and provide the child with an explanation. Explanations are important, because they help children make sense of the rules and regulations by which they must live. When rules make sense to a child, the rules are more likely to be honored than if they seem vague or come without explanation.

Also, by specifying what a child can do with a object such as the vase above - "Look at it" you are setting boundaries and at the same time giving him some freedom to explore. When phrased in this positive manner, the child does not hear that you are forbidding him to do something, he hears that you are giving him permission to explore. This works well on teenagers too. You just need to be a little more sophisticated with your request. You may say, for example: "Henry, if you return promptly at 10 p.m. you may have the privilege of using my car to go to the movie tomorrow." Technically you are still saying: "I'll let you use the car tomorrow if you don't stay out past 10:00 P.M. tonight," but the former suggestion works best because it focuses more on the privilege of taking the car to the movie rather than the limit of a 10:00 P.M. curfew.

10.N *Shame on you, you bad boy. You broke your aunt's vase.*

10.P *I can tell you feel pretty badly about breaking that vase. I bet Aunt Harriet feels pretty bad too. You are a good boy, but you have made a bad choice by disobeying me and touching and breaking Aunt Harriet's vase.*

"Shame on you" is perhaps one of the most harmful suggestions that we can give a child. Shame is devastating to healthy self-esteem, and is not to be mistaken for remorse or guilt. Remorse and guilt are quite different from shame, and can sometimes be productive emotions if we keep the feelings of guilt or remorse only long enough to promote learning and change. For example, we may feel guilty about an action that we took that hurt others, but if we learn from that mistake and see it as a growing experience that makes us stronger, self-respect remains intact.

Shame, on the other hand, is a much more destructive emotional state. It is more than just remorse for our deeds. It is self-remorse. Self-remorse or shame is extremely detrimental to a developing child's self-esteem or anyone's self-esteem for that matter. It makes a person feel badly not just for what he has done, but also for who he is. Many, if not most of us, were taught to shame ourselves as children. "You should be ashamed of yourself," was and still is a very common tactic to embarrass a child into conformity. As a consequence, we reach adulthood having grown very competent at shaming ourselves for the things we do that we or others assess as "wrong." We often carry the scars of shame (self-inflicted as well as other-inflicted) for the rest of our lives. Therefore, suggesting that your child should feel shame, with such shame conditioning phrases as: "shame on you," "for shame," or "you should be ashamed of yourself," is extremely counterproductive to the self-confidence and self-esteem you are striving to nurture and build in your children. If I may give you a positive suggestion - Remember to eliminate shame, both in word and in deed, from your repertoire of disciplinary skills. Remember to forget to use it on yourself too! Focus instead on ways in which you can empower your children to respect themselves and be proud of how they care for the world around them - For pride and self-respect are not only the antithesis of shame, but are significant attributes upon which a healthy personality thrives.

I suspect that the exercise above was not very difficult to do. You were probably fairly good at it too. Once you get the hang of it, positive verbal reinforcement is quite a stimulating experience. Redesigning negative conversations into positive ways of communicating is fun, mentally challenging, produces fast, affirmative results and makes us feel very good about being parents.

Quite often I have been asked by parents: "**If** positive verbal reinforcement is in fact a joyful, fun, stimulating experience, and is scientifically proven to produce the most affirmative results, why is it that the vast majority of people still use negative reinforcement and negative kinds of conversations to shape children's behaviors?"

The answer to this question is quite simple and can be explained by the following theory: We tend to continue to do something in the same manner in which we have been taught to do it, no matter how ineffective, unless we learn a new or more effective way of doing it. Essentially, we parent the way our parents parented us. Whether healthy or detrimental, we inherit a legacy of parenting skills that tend to accompany us into parenthood until we:

1. become conscious of our effective as well as ineffective parenting skills
2. replace the ineffective skills with effective ones

3. continue to practice these new parenting skills until they become a regular part of the healthy skills we will pass on to the generations that follow us.

Alice Miller in her brilliant work *For Your Own Good*[19] refers to the passing on of poor parenting skills as the "Poisonous Pedagogy." She too affirms that unless we reach out and discover better parenting skills we will continue to use some of the detrimental and ineffective ones that were handed down by former generations. I would like to state here that I know, and have heard of, many individuals from past generations who possessed exceptional parenting skills. However, according to anthropological studies of many different cultures these exceptional parents were not as predominant as those who lacked the distinctions to parent well.

I realize that this last statement may trigger some of you, but many mental health researchers and practitioners and the behavioral science community at large, believe that approximately 95% of all individuals were and are reared in what is considered a "dysfunctional environment." A dysfunctional environment is loosely defined as a environment which inhibits the healthy growth of its members.

When I first heard this statistic, I intellectually challenged it. I thought it must be inflated - ninety-five percent? Then I stopped to consider the lives of the people with which I have had frequent contact - family, friends, acquaintances and colleagues. I assess that the vast majority of people I knew - about 90% or so - (excluding my patients) possessed some form of life inhibiting emotional immaturity which I could track down to experiences within their family of origin.

---

[19] Alice Miller, <u>For Your Own Good</u> (New York: Farrar Straus, 1983), p. 140

Though this may indeed be a grim statistic, I have solid evidence that suggests the tide is turning and we are dawning upon an age of enlightenment for the family. Author Vicki Lansky has created a wonderful little book called *101 Ways to Make Your Child Feel Special*.[20] In it she exemplifies what is happening now to change the poisonous pedagogy by listing 101 ways in which we can support children in developing a strong sense-of-self and a feeling of joy about simply being alive. There are scores of other wonderful books, groups, organizations and experts out there who are optimistic and eager to support parents in our quest for the peaceful, joyful existence that we all deserve.

You can feel proud and confident that you too are working to create the new prototype of parenting - The Positive Pedagogy so to speak. Your efforts will blaze a trail and set a precedent for the highly effective, joyful and affirmative parenting skills that will assist all the children of the world in becoming fully functional individuals. Educators, counselors, ministers, day care providers or any influential individual in a child's life can benefit from healthy child development skills as well. Even those who do not have extensive contact with children, can greatly improve the quality of their lives and the lives of those around them by using these skills in caring for themselves and the world around them.

A word of caution: When practicing new parenting skills, you may at first encounter a bit of self-resistance or awkwardness. This is normal. You might think of it as a feeling very similar to trading in your old typewriter for a computer. For those of you who have done this, remember how you hated to get rid of the typewriter because it was so familiar, comfortable and predictable? But once you had become familiar with the computer and realized how

---

[20]Vicki Lansky, 101 Ways to Make Your Child Feel Special (Chicago, Comtempo, 1991)

much more efficient and easy it was to use, you wondered what ever took you so long to make the change.

The same holds true for developing new and more effective parenting skills. When exploring and attempting to use more positive parenting skills, use any resistance you have as an opportunity to learn new things about yourself and to grow from this knowledge. Remember life is a continual experience of growth. Remember, also that continuing to develop your own healthier personality is essential in helping your children to develop theirs. Positive conversation, positive reinforcement and a positive outlook are extraordinary tools for learning to grow as parents, as children and as individuals.

Refrigerator Post-it

1. There is a positive action to replace every negative action that occurs.

2. There is a positive word to replace every negative word that is spoken.

3. When we want our children to eliminate a certain behavior, before making the request, reflect upon what it is we want the child to do. Then speak the request from that point of reference. e.g. rather than saying: ***Stop throwing that ball inside.*** You could say: ***You may throw the ball outside or you may put it away. Balls are for outside play only!***

4. Key words and phrases to watch out for when making requests:

    Don't...
    Why don't you ... (unfavorable comparison)
    Never...
    You are so... (with an insult*)*
    You never...
    You always..
    I can't stand it when you....

5. Key words and phrases to use in making positive requests:

    You are so... (with a complement)
    Thank you for...
    Please do the following...
    I really appreciate it when you...
    I would appreciate it if you...
    I need you to do the following....

To label me is to negate me.

Soren Kierkegaard

Chapter 10

Labeling
(The Good, the Bad and the Ugly)

It has probably become apparent to you that I prefer to dwell within the realm of the positive. I feel however, that in order for us to achieve a deeper understanding of the effects that language has upon a child's life, we must devote time to the study of negative suggestion and its effect on the developing child.

I remember that as a child when someone teased me, I would repeat the often used phrase, "Sticks and stones may break my bones, but names will never hurt me." I also remember how those words would stick in my throat as I tried to stifle the tears of humiliation and sadness that longed to be expressed. I no doubt was trying to convince myself of their truth more than I was trying to convince the kids who were saying the hurtful things.

There is also a billboard on a highway I frequently travel that depicts a sad faced child with the phrase *"Words can hit as hard as fists."* This billboard was designed for those who read it to ponder how emotionally devastating the wrong words can be to a child's emerging self-esteem.

As I suggested earlier, the use of hurtful words and labels to shape children's behaviors and attitudes is extremely counterproductive and unfortunately all too prevalent in our society. One need only go to the corner market or neighborhood park to confirm this observation. As I suggested earlier, you and I are pioneers on a new and healthier journey into parenthood. As pioneers, we must brave the raised eyebrows and jeers of others who have not yet embraced the more loving, more gentle, more respectful - more enlightened ways of caring for children. I also envision that we will show them by example, that love, kindness and respect are parents' greatest allies in fostering a generation of individuals who will bring love, peace and harmony to themselves and to our planet.

Let us now move forward on our quest for peace and for a deeper understanding of the impact of language.

Dangerous Labels

Labels, According to Frank Taylor in his book, *The Pleasure of Their Company*, "may not only be perceived as truth but be acted upon as true. Labels can be made in fun, but endured in pain."[21]

One of the most fundamental messages that I strive to make in this book is that **What we tell our children they are, they become!** Occasionally when I have proposed this concept to parents, they have said something similar to what follows, "Oh, my calling Tiffany a bad girl didn't make her bad, she was bad long before I ever started calling her that. Ever since she was very little she has been nothing but trouble. She was always crying as an infant and boy did she have one awful case of the "Terrible Two's." Terrible Tiffany is what we call her, and she was like that since the day she was born."

I certainly have compassion and understanding for parents like Tiffany's who believe that Tiffany came into this word with a predisposition for "badness." Let us look however, at a likely scenario that sets families like Tiffany's up, not only to believe their children are bad or terrible, but to continue to label them as such. I will use the concept of the "Terrible Two" syndrome to show how a child's normal behavior can be misinterpreted as bad or terrible. Let us also discover how by gaining a better understanding of the age of two, or for that matter, any age, we can prevent ourselves and our children from ever falling into the "Terrible Twos, Threes, Twelves or Twenties trap." Even if you no longer have children in these age ranges, you can benefit by sharing this information with those around you who are still struggling or may be struggling with these issues in the future.

---

[21] Ibid., p. 107.

I will not attempt to make parenting a two-year-old sound like a leisurely walk down a country road. We all know that parenting or teaching a child of this age is at times challenging and highly frustrating. I will testify however, that parenting a two-year-old is also very rewarding, exhilarating, loads of fun and an overall joyful experience. Parenting a two-year-old is a lot like learning to drive a car or learning a new job. We can take the frustrations and challenges and use them to improve our current level of competency, and we can celebrate when we have mastered a new level of understanding and skill.

I firmly believe that there is no such thing as a terrible two-year-old. They are all **terrific** two-year-olds in my eyes. One way to dispel the terrible two myth is to look more closely at those behaviors that we are actually calling terrible. Almost all of those "terrible" behaviors are actually behaviors that, if channeled properly, will strengthen the child's self-esteem and give him the confidence and courage to go out and take on anything that the world has to offer him. Let's take a look at the terrific two's more closely.

Before the age of two, you might say the child perceives himself as an appendage of his parents. Like your arms and legs, the infant thinks he is literally attached to you. At about the age of two, however he begins to realize that he is an entity unto himself, a totally separate and unique being. At the same time, he is discovering that moving about in space is much easier than it was just a few months ago. He can walk and may even run. Consequently the dog in the yard across the street is a lot more accessible than it was when he was one and a half years of age.

To a two-year-old, this new found knowledge is both frightening and exhilarating. He now realizes that he is a separate individual from you, and this discovery of his separateness sometimes makes him cling to you more closely than before. At other times he explores the boundaries of his separateness by running as fast and as far away from you as he can without looking back. In other words, he is awakening to, testing and exploring his own individuality and awakening to the many possibilities that are out there for discovery.

When testing his freedom of movement, he is often like a colt first learning to gallop. He is off and running, and if we allow him, he will run all the way to the end of the fence line an attempt to jump over it. Perhaps the most challenging part of parenting a two-year-old is allowing him freedom to explore, and at the same time, lovingly and consistently enforcing boundaries. At times, we must also allow him the freedom to push against those boundaries we create for him, so that he can learn what consequences or opportunities await him on the other side.

What the typical two-year-old needs is:

- lots of space to explore the world around him
- guidelines and boundaries set for him
- freedom to test the boundaries from time to time
- reassurance, comfort and guidance when he does go off exploring and testing

I am not just referring to the physical space in which he moves, but I am referring to the emotional space as well. He needs to feel free to cry when he's hurt, to scream (a little) when he is excited, to feel anger when he is mad, to laugh when something is funny and to smile at that which pleases him. He is beginning to understand that there are emotions swelling up from inside of him, and he needs a safe place to express them.

At the same time he needs to learn that his emotions must not be allowed to hurt others. He must be allowed to feel and express emotions such as anger, but at the same time learn the appropriate ways in which to express them. He must also be told that hitting another human being is not an appropriate expression of anger - So we need to consistently model this rule as well. He must be allowed and encouraged to laugh often when things are funny, but must also be taught not to laugh at the expense of others. (like in church where his laughter is usually disruptive to others.

In light of the information I presented above, we can truthfully say that many parental duties of a two-year-old are challenging in nature. None of them however can truly be considered terrible. Demanding - yes, but terrible-no way. Even with all its challenges, the Terrific Two's should still engender more rewards for parents than conflicts-Like the way he rests his head on your shoulder and wraps his arms around you when he's tired, and the way he squeals with excitement when his sees an airplane or a balloon overhead, or the way that his tiny hand melds into yours when you hold it, and the way he smiles at you when you have just said something loving to him.

How we perceive our two-year-old children is dictated by our moods, current situations and personal history. Much like Prisilla and Sandy in the earlier chapter, you can allow the things that are difficult about your child to color the way you feel about him, or you can continue to re-center on the things that make him precious and a unique expression of joy. Tiffany's parents, like many, dwelled upon the things that were difficult and failed to see how Tiffany's challenging behaviors were really a prelude to her healthy mental and physical growth. As a result, Tiffany became a self-fulfilling prophesy for her parents and developed behaviors that reinforced the terrible label that was placed upon her at two years of age. Had her family assessed and defined Tiffany's two-year-old behavior as normal and healthy, Tiffany's chances of developing into a healthy, well adjusted individual would have been much greater. When I become really frustrated with my own children's challenging behavior, I often remember the words of a dear friend: "If you give them lots of love, the children you can do the least with, will make you the most proud."

Even when you suspect that your child's difficult behavior is genetically and permanently encoded within his DNA, you can both still benefit by seeing the difficult behavior as an opportunity to learn and to grow. My daughter Claire possesses a personality trait that will serve her well in this life, but at times I find somewhat challenging. She is a very strong willed child. You might hear others refer to or label this trait as "pig headed", "stubborn" or "aggressive." Because I perceive my husband, myself and my son as fairly flexible, easy going individuals, I have entertained the thought that this strong willed aspect of her personality might just have been inherited from her paternal grandfather who died before she was born. I also believe that I may have fostered this behavior in some way without being aware of it.

All things considered, we don't know where her extreme determination to do things her way comes from, but I am convinced that it is deeply imbedded in her psyche. Over time and thanks to the support of her wonderfully enlightened kindergarten teacher, Mrs. Whitaker, I have come to see her "strong willed" nature as a gift and an asset. Mrs. Whitaker contends that her strong willed nature is the catalyst for her above average level of task commitment in school and will likely make her a strong leader in the future. On several occasions, her teacher has brought to my attention that no matter how frustrated, she will stick to a task until she has completed it, and rally the support of others as needed-but she does not give up or abandon her cause. I have since noticed this determination and commitment at home as well.

She and I have also made great strides in channeling her willfulness into productive avenues. I now know that in carefully nurturing and channeling this trait, I am rearing a child who will have the courage and **will**, as my friend Wendy put it, to say no to drugs or alcohol when peer pressure is at its peak. I also have several new ways to hold her willfulness - *budding leadership qualities, perseverance and persistence* to name a few. These labels certainly do more to enhance her self-esteem than "stubborn" or "pig headed" ever would, and they help me to continue to view aspects of this behavior as an asset. I also believe that by dwelling upon the positive aspects of her willfulness, this personality trait will serve her very well in life, and will be used to serve others.

In short, viewing our children's normal, age appropriate behaviors and unique personality traits in a positive light does a tremendous service for our child's developing character. Unfortunately, even when you keep your conversations, labels and attitudes positive, other uninformed people may not. It is at these times that you need to rally behind your child, even if it causes discomfort for you and the person making the negative assessment. To put it in the words of another of my wise friends, Mary Simmons, "It is our job to be our children's greatest advocates."

Several years ago, while at the local market with Claire, I was called to be her advocate. As often happens in grocery stores, an "I want" battle broke out between a mother and child at the check out line. This time that Mom and child was us. Apparently, Claire wanted to eat her bag of strawberries before the cashier could weigh and record them. As I steadfastly insisted on taking the bag, she verbally and physically protested. The protest (you know the type) could be heard by shoppers way back in the dairy section of the grocery store, but I managed to confiscate the bag anyway. As I handed the strawberries to the cashier however, the cashier shook her head from side to side in a disapproving fashion and said; "That brat certainly has a mind of her own."

Aroused by this cashier's total lack of concern for our feelings, I quickly came to Claire's defense. In the most polite but firm tone I could muster at that moment, I said, "She is not a brat. Just like you, she is a precious child of God. I may not approve of her behavior right now, but she is often very courteous and loving. As far as having a mind of her own, I'm really grateful for that, because I certainly wouldn't want her to have anyone else's!"

Though I often find confronting people difficult, in this instance I felt it necessary to let Claire know that as her mother, I would not allow another adult to call her names or ridicule her in my presence. After all, it is part of a parent's job to make a young child feel safe and secure in the world. Unfortunate as it may be, defending them against an adult's insensitive remarks and/or physical outbursts is sometimes part of our job. I am also teaching Claire, by example, to advocate for herself someday when someone insults her or harms her in any way.

Thus, we not only need to choose words carefully ourselves, but we need to be aware of the negative labels and remarks that other people try to place upon our children as well. We need to be very cautious as to how we and others label children, whether to their faces, to others in front of them and even behind their backs, because labels tend to stick. Since labels stick, we want to assign children lots of positive and uplifting labels that will stick to their subconscious as well as conscious image of who they are and what they are capable of becoming. Even if you have to use your imagination a bit to find the right labels, rise up to the challenge and your children will too.

I realize that there are some of you who might protest the use of labels at all-contending that whether perceived as good or bad, labels should not be used. Let me say that I appreciate this philosophy, but I believe, as humans, we instinctively categorize and label in an effort to make sense of the world in which we live. We must also remember that children categorize even more than adults. Therefore, we must provide children with good labels about themselves, so that they can have lots of positive labels to add to their self-concepts file-a file they will draw upon for the rest of their lives.

Lastly, there is never a good reason to label or call your child such things as bad, stupid, slow, ignorant or lazy. These labels only serve to reinforce bad, stupid, slow, ignorant or lazy behaviors. When we call a child bad or lazy, it is like making one of those "always" statements that we discussed earlier. The child who hears an adult call him bad or lazy, has an internal conversation that goes something like this, "Because I did a bad thing, I am (always) a bad person." Because I acted lazy just now, I must (always) be a lazy person." Sound familiar? Every child has their moments of misbehavior, lack of motivation and slowness of wit. If we harp upon these behaviors we will see them appear more often. They become self-fulfilling prophecies for both us and our children. If however, we segregate the behavior from the child, by saying, "You are a good person, but you did a bad thing," we are distinguishing the behavior from the self, and the self-esteem remains intact.

If by chance your child seems extremely lazy or extremely disruptive, you might look for the circumstances in his life that have contributed to his lack of motivation or his acting out behaviors. If he is hard to motivate, does he often hear phrases like, "You can't do that," "Here let me show you the RIGHT way to do it," "Why can't you be more like your sister?" If he has a consistent pattern of acting out behavior, does he get the right amount of **healthy** loving attention at home? Do you or the other significant adults in his life routinely take time to play with him and talk with him about his concerns, hopes and dreams? Does he receive messages that say "We enjoy having you around." Is he taken out to special events or outings of his choice, and do those who love him make it a habit to stop, look and listen to what he has to say?

If you answered "no" to some of the preceding questions, please resist the urge to shame yourself. Use this insight instead as an opportunity to begin to foster healthy, encouraging conversations with those you love. Parents that I have worked with continue to be amazed at how resilient and responsive their children are to loving and caring words. As a fifty-eight-year-old friend of mine can attest, even adult children can be extremely resilient and forgiving. This particular friend spent all of his prime parenting years as a self-centered alcoholic. He has five adult children ranging from thirty-eight to twenty two-years of age who also suffered from his illness. After going through the *Twelve Step* program himself, he and his five children went through family counseling together. As a result of this joint family effort, the children have forgiven him for his absence and emotional neglect in their earlier lives, and are now enjoying an emotionally healthy and growing family relationship. My friend now preaches to others that it is rarely too late to begin to be a loving, supportive parent to your children, and the energy you put into doing so will come back to you one hundred fold.

Exercise 23

Below, on the left column, list several personality traits your child possesses that you have assessed as negative. In the right column re-examine and rephrase this trait in a way that views it as a positive one.

e.g. Pat is lazy.   Pat's laid back, type B, relaxed

_____   _____

e.g. Sarah is sassy.   Sarah speaks up for herself.

_____   _____

_____   _____

_____   _____

_____   _____

_____   _____

_____   _____

_____   _____

Now reflect on the exercise above, and write a paragraph about the new possibilities that might open up for you and your child if you began to see and speak about these personality traits in a positive way.

_____

_____

_____

_____

_____

_____

_____

_____

Refrigerator Post-it

1. Whether positive or negative in nature, labels stick.

2. Parents have awesome power to inspire or disable their children by labeling them.

3. Most personality traits that we assess as negative also have a positive side.

4. A few examples of the two sides of a personality trait are:

<u>**Negative Side / Positive Side**</u>
stubborn/determined
arrogant/confident
shy/reflective
hyper/motivated
lazy/relaxed
bossy/enrolling or leader
impatient/eager

The health, vitality and happiness
of the family is the yardstick by
which a man, woman and society
should measure success and failure.

Sam Keen

Chapter 11

Keeping Conversations Positive

In *As A Man Thinkith,* 19th century Englishman and philosopher, James Allen, wrote:

> *The aphorism* (quote) *"As a man thinketh in his heart so is he," not only embraces the whole of man's being, but is so comprehensive as to reach out to every condition and circumstance of his life.* ***A man is literally what he thinks, his character being the complete sum of all his thoughts.***

What we think about ourselves today was often what was thought about and spoken to us as children-so it stands to reason that what we think about our children today is what they may become tomorrow. Stop and listen carefully for those messages that have been recorded in your mind from your own childhood-the ones you presently speak to and about yourself and your children. Listen for and keep the healthy messages that help to foster your self-confidence and the self-confidence of your children. Listen for and eliminate the messages that you assess as unhealthy and detrimental to your families' healthy growth and development. As you listen to yourself thinking negatively about yourself and your loved ones, simply STOP yourself from speaking or thinking them and refuse to play those old recordings any longer. (You may also want to refer to the section on the STOP technique when doing so.) You can begin to erase the self-effacing and child-effacing tapes by affirming something like what follows:

> ***From this day forward, I will speak to and about myself and my children in loving, kind, and compassion ways.***

Exercise 24

List four negative messages you received in your childhood that you want to eliminate:

1. _____

2. _____

3. _____

4. _____

List four positive messages with which you will replace the ones above:

1. _____

2. _____

3. _____

4. _____

Exercise 25

List four negative messages that you give to your children that you want to discontinue:

1. _____

2. _____

3. _____

4. _____

List 4 positive messages you will give to your children that will replace the ones on the previous page:

1. _____

2. _____

3. _____

4. _____

When we keep our thoughts and speech positive and optimistic, we become our own and our children's greatest advocates. What's more, our positive thinking transcends ourselves and our children and has a life altering rippling effect on the entire world.

When you spill a cup of coffee on yourself do you silently speak, "Oh, how stupid," or "what an idiot I am?" If you do use this harsh self-talk, chances are you heard these words when you spilled something as a child. Chances are you may even be saying things like that to your own child. Next time you catch yourself thinking negatively, STOP, and speak to yourself or your child like you would be speaking to your very best friend. How would you respond to your best friend if she spilled her drink on your table? Now respond to yourself and your child in the same way. You will find harmony and peace in your home when you begin to speak to yourself and to those you love with the same dignity, kindness and respect that you do to the cherished others in your life.

We have a lot vested in maintaining a healthy and respectful relationship with ourselves and in speaking to ourselves with the kindness and respect we deserve as human beings. There is also no other way to a happy and peaceful life but through self-love.

Positive Thought Becomes Positive Action

When we think positively, we speak positively. When we speak positively, positive action results. I believe that we can accomplish all good things for ourselves and for our loved ones with loving and compassionate thought and speech. Even when your child is about to leave home for school with what looks like an eagle's nest in the back of his hair, you can suggest that he will look and feel his best if he combs it out. Or you might suggest that others will appreciate his efforts to groom himself, and so will you. If you have a lot of energy on having his hair groomed before he leaves, you can also kindly but firmly suggest that he will be allowed to leave when his hair is combed.

A kind but firm way of speaking to our children is a lot more effective than a disrespectful one, because we show that we honor the child as an individual. Loving and caring communication will provide your child with the positive motivation that he will need to work within the guidelines of your home and those of society. Belittling, threatening, humiliating or angry words like, "Your hair looks ridiculous, and I'll be damned if you are leaving this house until you comb it" are often ineffective, because it makes a child defensive, closing their minds to further communication and is an assault to their integrity and developing self-esteem. As I have said before, acknowledgment and encouragement are much more effective at shaping behavior and attitude than criticism, humiliation and punishment.

Ways to Keep Conversation Positive and Productive

In my former place of employment, I worked with a group of ten individuals. We had an unspoken rule that whenever anyone was trying to give themselves or anyone else a suggestion that sounded negative in nature, it was subtly brought to their attention. Once brought to their attention, the person usually reframed his or her suggestion into a more positive one. This plan worked very well for us, and our office was a cheerful, uplifting environment in which to work.

I encourage you to experiment with this "check and balance" system in your own home, school or office. Let the kids in your life in on the action too. Kids love to have the opportunity to help adults. It makes them feel needed and important. Once you have your plan in action, you will notice that even pointing out negative suggestions can be done in a positive way. You can say for example: "I'd like you to rephrase that suggestion in a more positive way, Billy?" Very young children can give parents a simple reminder such as: "Dad can you please say that more nicely?" Even if your home or work place is already a very uplifting place to be, you will notice an even higher level of functioning once everyone becomes aware of the way in which they speak to themselves and others.

I am not suggesting here that you become Pollyanna's - or look at the world with blinders on and deny painful moods. There are valid reasons to experience and express moods, feelings and emotions such as sadness, anger, fatigue and frustration. To simply act as if nothing is wrong would be to deny ourselves the right to communicate and work through our feelings in appropriate ways. The key phrase here though is *to communicate our feelings in appropriate ways*. We can be hurt, angry, frustrated, humiliated, depressed or sad and still manage to communicate our feelings to the appropriate people in constructive ways.

While striving to communicate our feelings however, it is unproductive to explode with hostile aggression or to ridicule or condemn another person. Unfortunately, this is an all too prevalent form of communication. It's another one of those family and societal traits that have been passed on from generation to generation without much thought given to its consequences.

If you are like the majority of us and find it difficult at times to express anger and frustration without losing your sense of balance, or without wanting to verbally attack the other person, here are a few points to keep in mind.

1. Omit "always" and "never" statements from your conversations, unless they are followed by a complement, such as; "Thanks, you always remember to bring me flowers on my birthday."

2. Resist the urge to ridicule or verbally attack anyone at anytime. You can always say what needs to be said in a respectful but firm manner. Essentially, maintain your own dignity and respect the dignity of others. Remember even those who we feel to be ruthless or hostile in manner were once innocent children who were likely deprived of the opportunity to learn compassionate and loving behavior.

3. Remember, hurtful words said in anger can rarely be retracted, and they often leave deep scars.

4. Barring those few individuals with pathological needs for violent conflict, the real reasons most of us get angry and argue is to resolve conflict and make requests. Verbal attacks however, put the person being accused or attacked in a defensive posture and makes it extremely difficult for them to hear the real requests behind the negative accusations.

If your goal is to communicate that which made you hurt or angry, you will best be heard if you make your requests and statements in a clear, direct but dignified manner, and refrain from sarcasm, belittling statements and other verbal daggers. To accomplish this, begin with "I" statements rather than "You" statements.

"You" statements such as: *You make me really angry when you are late for dinner* tend to make others feel attacked. This encourages defensive conversations. "I" statements like: *I get very upset when you are late for dinner, because ....*, work best at accomplishing peaceful results, because "I" statements are heard by others as a statement of your needs rather than their liabilities. With "I" statements you are assuming responsibility for your own needs and moods, and this allows the other individual to focus on your request. Otherwise, the individual hearing a statement, like "You make me angry", feels compelled to defend himself and is consequently distracted from your real request - "I would like you to come home on time for dinner, because...."

Requests come in many disguises. When we speak our requests in anger, or so vaguely that the listener may not hear or understand them, we deny ourselves and the listener the opportunity to respond effectively to our requests. This is especially true in communication between parents and children. Children need requests made to them as directly as possible. As I stated in a previous chapter, a direct request speaks the request in the most overt, plain, clear and concise manner possible. When we can achieve this highly evolved way of communication with our loved ones, we increase our chances that all of our communications will be beneficial to those who are party to them.

In the next chapter I will elaborate on the more subtle ways we communicate our requests, our suggestions and our moods to those around us. We need to remain very alert to these more subtle forms of communication, because the subtleties of language are also very powerful in shaping the developing personality and in shaping behavior. In the following pages, I will show you why.

In the next chapter, you will learn to identify the more subtle and covert requests which we all hear and speak on a daily basis. For now, try exercise 26 to test your listening of convert requests. See if you can identify unspoken requests and concerns below. (There are no right or wrong answers.)

Exercise 26

Find the hidden request or concern within each of the covert requests below and rephrase the request or concern in a clear and respectful manner.

1. "You're always waiting till the last minute to get things done!"

_____

_____

_____

_____

2. "Fred, do you really think you need to be eating a second helping of cheesecake?"

_____

_____

_____

_____

3. "Go ahead and wear that ridiculous outfit, and see the reaction you get from your friends ."

_____

_____

_____

_____

Refrigerator Post-it

1. Thoughts produce things! Our actions are a result of our thoughts. We create our reality through what we think all day long and we help our children create their realities as well.

2. We are the only person with the authority to choose the conversations we have with ourselves.

3. The way we speak and the words we speak to our children are the way they will speak to themselves.

4. Use the STOP technique to eliminate negative self-talk or negative thoughts about our children.

    e.g. (To self) *"You idiot, how stupid to spill coffee on your pants."*

    STOP

    change to: *"I see that I'm still human , and I'm finally O.K. with that!*

5. Unless spoken as a prelude to a complement, avoid *always and never* statements.

6. Make all request of others with dignity and with clarity.

You are all children of light..

1 Thessalonians 5:5

Chapter 12

Indirect Verbal
Suggestion

In this section, we will explore indirect verbal suggestions. Indirect verbal suggestions can be inferred or implied suggestions, or they can be suggestions that are spoken at but not directly to another. I would like to begin by first discussing the suggestion which is spoken in the presence of someone but not directly to another. If the message is negative in nature (which is usually the case) then I call it a *Passive/Aggressive* suggestion or statement. This type of indirect suggestion or covert request occurs when someone speaks to a third party or speaks out loud to themselves, but intends for you to overhear the conversation. In this situation the result is not genuine communication but ineffective communication that causes the listener to feel indignant. The passive/aggressive statement causes anger and feelings of indignation because it is a cowardly action. It is cowardly because the speaker chooses not to confront the person directly, but chooses instead to attack from behind so to speak. This kind of attack tends to rob the other person of some dignity since the space to make a complaint or provide an explanation or defense is taken away. The correct response is to make the conversation a direct conversation by speaking directly to the "subject" so that he may be allowed to respond with honesty and dignity to your request or concern.

Just recently while being served my meal at a local fast food restaurant, I was struck by the harshness of a passive/aggressive statement that was directed at me. After receiving my food tray at the service counter of this restaurant, I turned to walk away. Because the women behind me was closer than I had thought, I bumped into her and accidentally spilled some of my soft drink onto the leg of her pants. Instead of directly telling me that she was upset that I spilled my drink on her, this individual turned to the man with her and proclaimed in an angry tone: "I hate people who don't look where they are going."

Since I did not realize that she was standing so close behind me, and certainly did not intend to spill my drink, I quickly excused my behavior as not being rude, since, in my opinion, rudeness must stem from an intentional act. I also suggested to her that had she referred to me directly and with even a small degree of kindness and respect, I would have certainly apologized and may have even offered to buy her meal for her, which I sincerely may have done for someone who had been nicer about the whole situation.

Her passive aggressive manner made it easy for me to defend myself, and consequently failed to bring forth any result that may have been satisfactory to her. This type of communication almost always tends to provoke negative feelings on the part of the recipient. At best, a passive/aggressive comment will be ignored. At worst, a passive/aggressive indirect comment will provoke individuals with a confrontational nature to attack back. I have certainly seen this happen more than once.

Another form of indirect communication which is spoken at but not to someone is what I call the *Third Party Conversation*. Here an individual, usually someone who has been taught to shy away from any confrontation, will speak to a third party in order to relay a message to the second. An all too frequently used third party message occurs when a spouse uses a child as a buffer to relay a message to the other spouse. It goes something like this: The father enters the house some time after he has been expected home. The mother who is frustrated with this situation, but does not have the courage and/or skills to express this frustration directly to the father says: "I see your father has come home late for dinner again. We've already eaten so I guess he will just have to fend for himself. Right, kids?" The real travesty of this kind of suggestion is the "emotional garbage" that it dumps on the kids. Does the child really need to be a part of this argument? Should the child be expected to side with one parent or the other? Certainly not, but children are often unintentionally used as pawns, as emotional buffers between parents who sometimes lack the courage or skills to communicate directly.

Another way in which a third party suggestion can be detrimental to someone (especially a child) is when we make a negative comment about someone, in front of them, but not directly to them - Slightly different from the example above, the person we are speaking about is standing beside us engaged in the conversation with us, but we are speaking to someone else about them almost as if they were not present. This is often done between adults in the presence of a child. I observed one such conversation at a party that has remained with me till this day.

In the situation, a lady that I will call Mrs. Burn was standing in conversation with her son, Bobby, and with another woman whom I will call Mrs. Chen. At one point in the conversation, Mrs. Burn declared to Mrs. Chen, "Bobby is so terrible at reading. I think we are going to have to have him evaluated for dyslexia. I just don't know what's wrong with him. We have never had anyone with reading disabilities in our family before."

Though the third party suggestion above is somewhat mild compared to a lot of other comments that I have heard parents speak in front of their children, I will never forget the dismayed and disbelieving look on Bobby's face. It seemed to be saying, "I can't believe my mother would betray me by telling the world how terrible I am at reading." - I must admit, even if the child wasn't thinking that, I sure was. It was totally inappropriate and insensitive of her to speak about her son in front of him and as if he wasn't there. Furthermore, I feel that there is no time when a negative suggestion has a stronger impact than when a parent makes a derogatory comment about his or her child in front of another person.

Because the child feels that the parent has betrayed his confidence and emotionally abandoned him, I think that this form of negative suggestion has the most damaging emotional impact of all. The child begins to mistrust a parent who speaks poorly of him in front of others.

It is therefore important that you carefully watch what you say about your child to others, whether in their presence or not. Even when your children are very small and you think that they will be unable to understand you, assume that they can. Research has shown that infants can understand every word we say on some level of their mind, consciously, subconsciously or unconsciously. The bottom line on negative passive/aggressive and negative third party conversations is to strive to eliminate them from your repertoire of communication skills. They have no place in sound, healthy communication.

Conversely, positive, third party conversations can be healthy and assuring to the developing child. In one of the earlier chapters, I gave you one example of a positive third party comment when I recalled the situation with my friend and her four children at the health club nursery. Another example that comes to mind was one that I witnessed recently at school. While at a PTA meeting, I overheard a mother speaking to her child's teacher while in the presence of her child. The teacher was complimenting the child and mother on how well the child had been doing in school. The mother thanked the teacher for the compliment, and then replied; "Well , if he works half as hard at school, as he does at home then I am not at all surprised that he is doing well."

As you read her comment, you might think that her praise was nothing terrific, but the thing that impressed me most was that she said it. Sadly, I typically don't hear words of acknowledgment about one's children coming from parents, while in the presence of their children. However, I have become weary at other times listening to parents brag about their children when the children are not around. I am sure I have done my fair share of this as well. I would like to propose, however that for the sake of our children's self-esteem and for the sake of all the weary listeners, we learn to curtail our bragging when the children are not around (except to grandparents of course), and instead brag about our children while they are present. I assure you, this won't make them conceited, but it well make them confident.

It was the opinion of my late father, and many other individuals of his time, that compliments spoken by a father to his children were inappropriate. Vicki Lansky wrote in *101 Ways to Make Your Child Feel Special:* "We have only to go back one or two generations to hear that praising a child or encouraging pride in a child would foster conceit and lack of humility."[22]

Because my father adhered so strongly to this belief, it was not until his death that I ever knew he had given me a compliment. It was actually at his funeral that a good friend and employee of his told me how proud my father was of me and how often he had spoken of my successes. At first I stared at this man with disbelief, but then just knowing the nature of this gentlemen, I realized that he had no motive to lie. I had never before known that my father was proud of my accomplishments. He had always been too fearful of fostering conceit to tell me.

I love my father dearly, and have found it difficult to share this story, but I do so with a message to you. It is my personal request that you do not make your children wait until you are gone for them to realize just how proud you are of their accomplishments. Tell them now, and tell them often. At times, tell them in front of others. Let them experience the wonderful feeling of parental approval now, so that they do not have to continue looking for it as adults. Nothing you can say is quite as bolstering to a child's self-esteem as when you sincerely say something complimentary about him in the presence of others. H. Jackson Brown put it nicely in his work *Life's Little Instruction Book*, when in suggestion #373 he advised: *Let your children overhear you saying complimentary things about them to other adults.*[23]

---

[22]Vicki Lansky, <u>101 Ways to Make Your Child Feel Special</u> (Chicago: Contemporary Books, 1991)

[23]H. Jackson Brown, <u>Life's Little Instruction Book</u> (Nashville: Ruthledge Hill, 1991), p. 373.

Become your children's greatest allies, give them compliments, in front of them, to others.

Implied Indirect Suggestions

Indirect suggestions are not limited to those suggestions we intend another to overhear, or suggestions that are spoken in the presence of someone but not directly to them. Indirect suggestion is also comprised of suggestions that are spoken specifically to an individual but have an inferred, insinuated or implied meaning. Let us look at a few examples of implied indirect suggestion.

Positive Implied Suggestion: I bet you are very proud of the "B" you got in reading today.
Implication: I am proud of the "B" you got in reading, and you should be too.

Negative Implied Suggestion: Are you going to enter THAT THING in the art contest?
Implication: I don't think THAT THING is good enough to enter into the art contest, therefore I question your judgment.

Though the message in both examples was only implied, they were still loud and clear. Implied suggestions can get a lot more subtle than this and still be very powerful. Therefore be conscious of what your conversations are implying, for your child may not consciously understand the suggestion, but will hear it on a deeper subconscious level of the mind.

It is because Negative Implied Suggestions have such a profound impact, that I advocate you speak most of your requests in as direct a way as possible. There are times however when more subtle suggestions are in order, and there are certain children who sometimes respond better to indirect positive suggestion. My daughter Claire is an excellent example of a child who often responds better to indirect positive suggestion. Since Claire has a strong need to control her personal environment, my husband and I have learned to work around this.

Now, we can tell our easy going Matthew to "Please clean your room" and without a lot of discussion he will. It takes a bit of coaxing however, to get Claire to do the same. Our best chance at getting Claire to clean her room might be to invite her to feel that she has initiated the idea. I might say: Claire, your friend Debbie is coming over this afternoon to play. What do you think you need to do to prepare for her visit? Though ideally she would respond ,"I could clean my room Mommy." She doesn't often do that, so I continue by saying: Do you think that organizing the toys and things in your room might make Debbie happy when she comes to play?"

On a good day and at some point, she will agree that cleaning her room before entertaining her guest is a good idea. She will think it is a good idea, because she feels that it was her idea. I never came right out and asked her to clean her room like I did Matthew, but the result was the same. Her room was cleaned.

Now I certainly do not use creative conversation every time I want Claire to obey my requests. Nor do I think it would be in her best interest to do so, but there are certain things, like cleaning her room, that I feel are best negotiated through the art of indirect positive suggestion.

Alternative Suggestions

If done positively, another successful way to speak a request to a child is through an alternative suggestion. A gentleman I worked with tells a story of how he used to inspire his son to do chores around the house without protest. He calls this strategy an "alternative suggestion." The way the alternative suggestion works is that you give your child a choice of chores. My friend uses the following example as an illustration. He would approach his son and say: "Son, would you like to clean out the attic for me today, or would you like to take out the garbage?" I'm sure it comes as no surprise that the son chose to take out the garbage. Most children will choose the chore that they perceive to be the easiest. However, in the unlikely event that your child may chose the more difficult, then you get a bonus that day.

If indirect suggestion can apparently move mountains by getting a willful child to clean her room or a son needing motivation to take out the garbage, when then should indirect suggestion not be used?

There are many instances when indirect suggestion should not be used - every time it has the potential to physically or emotionally hurt someone else. Since indirect suggestion often goes straight to the subconscious mind of a child undetected by the conscious mind, the potential for damage is greater. An example of a dangerous indirect suggestion might occur in a hypothetical situation where an angry five year-old boy has just thrown a plate across the room that has shattered in pieces. The mother, in an all too frequent and frustrated tone tells her son once again, that he is "just like his father." Though the boy is simply acting out a particular behavior that he has seen work for his father, (his masculine role model), the mother assumes he is destined to be as his father is.

The above suggestion is a dangerous suggestion to this child, because his father is an alcoholic, does not provide the family with financial assistance and is prone to physical domestic violence. Therefore, by making this ungrounded assessment about her son's plate throwing, she may have inadvertently watered the seeds of alcoholism, abuse and neglect that had already been planted in this innocent child's subconscious mind.

If on the other hand, she continually nourishes the concept that he will rise above his father's dysfunctional behaviors and she also provides him with appropriate role models to support him in doing so, he is likely to listen to her positive suggestions and become a healthier adult than his father.

By the same token, if you tell your child he is great with numbers, you are suggesting to your child that he is good at math. Every time he sits down to take a math test, his subconscious mind will recall your suggestion, and his chances of success will be much greater than if you told him that you yourself did horribly at math and you think he may have inherited your poor math skills. Remember, children's subconscious minds are hungry for nourishing thoughts and suggestions. Give them an inch of compliment and they will take a mile. I have worked with children whose learning abilities were greatly improved simply by my suggesting to them, sometimes in a hypnotic state, that they could learn the material easily and effortlessly, and by instructing parents to reinforce these positive suggestions at home.

Whether direct or indirect, affirmative suggestions for learning improvement or for behavior improvement work wonders with children. Just the other day, for example, my daughter Claire was having a difficult time in school learning her address, so right at bed time I suggested to her sleepy little mind that she would remember her current address for at least as long as we lived in our home. I also suggested that she would remember to say her full address upon awakening in the morning. About 4:30 A.M. the next morning she came to my bed and told me her address. When I asked her what she was doing up so early, she said that she had gotten up to use the bathroom but needed to tell me her address first.

In the last few days, I have quizzed her on her address several times, and she continues to say it without effort. In my profession and in my home life, I see and hear evidence of how well positive suggestion works almost on a daily basis. It is often the first and only option I need to use to improve my children's performance in school and at home.

Teasing, Sarcasm and Humor

I would like to touch briefly on the indirect suggestions given to children through teasing, sarcasm and humor. Adults can often detect sarcasm and teasing or humor in conversation - children, especially children under the age of eight or nine, often do not. As a result, children often mistake for fact, remarks intended to humor them or the adults speaking to them. Teasing is humor that is directed at a child, but often done with the intention of entertaining adults. In sadness and frustration, I have all too often witnessed the screams and cries of a child who is the pawn of another person's insensitive use of humor. Teasing is usually only fun for the person doing the teasing.

Teasing is often upsetting and humiliating to a child, because they lack the experience and the emotional development to understand the intent. Adults often think it is funny when a child is frightened by some absurd fantasy that is being conjured up. Frankly, there is nothing funny about frightening a child. I realize that adults rarely tease children as a conscious act of violence, but in my opinion, it **IS** an act of violence and insensitivity to ever tease a child until they cry or seem frightened.

Adult humor and sarcasm are often too sophisticated for small children. When misunderstood for fact, a sarcastic or humorous but untrue remark can be a very powerful suggestion. Just recently, at my son's school fair, a friend offered him a *Mountain Dew* soft drink. Noticing that Matthew was sweating and thirsty, I asked him why he did not accept the offer of the drink. Before responding, he looked around and over his shoulders then shyly remarked; "Don't you know Mom that the yellow dye in *Mountain Dew* stunts your growth." Though I tried to assure Matthew that this rumor was unfounded, he insisted that it was true. "Just ask Uncle Bill," he said, and then added, "Uncle Bill knows everything."

Though I don't think any permanent damage has occurred in Matthew's development from believing his Uncle Bill's attempt at humor, I have to wonder what other stories might Matthew have believed that could have given him some warped sense of reality. What if his Uncle Bill had told him that he were dumb or weak, or he had told him that certain races of people or intellectually superior to others? Would he have believed those things as passionately as he believes that *Mountain Dew* inhibits growth? I would not have considered that my very bright nine-year-old would have believed the absurd humor of his Uncle's statement, but it brought me back quickly to the realization of how vulnerable all children are to the remarks of those individuals that they hold as knowledgeable. I encourage you to check in with your children and think before you speak those humorous remarks that, if believed by your children, could create difficulty for them in the future. When you joke with them, assure that they know that you are in fact speaking humorously and that you do not intend them to take the remark seriously.

In essence, our children will thrive best if we engage in age appropriate humor with them and save our more sophisticated humor for older individuals who can appreciate it. We should also refrain from making negative jokes such as; "We are giving you up for adoption," even when we don't think the child may take it seriously - For you never know when he might. Lastly, we should joke only when it is not at the expense of another individual, and never as a way of covertly hurting someone - as sarcasm often does.

When our "humor" hurts, attacks or diminished someone in any way, it is a wrongful act. When we tease or make fun of someone, we may be speaking our anger at them in a covert way. Painful teasing and biting sarcasm can be an expression of hostility in disguise. Sarcasm can also be an attempt on the part of the speaker to elevate himself above another by making the other look inept, incompetent or stupid. With sarcasm, the speaker often tries to elevate himself by diminishing another. The speaker may have issues concerning his own self-esteem and uses sarcasm to alleviate (if only for a short time) the pain he feels about being inadequate. The hidden anger is that the speaker is angry with himself and/or the world because he feels inferior or inadequate in some or many ways. (Anger is always a response to a perceived threat and behind anger there is always a request or desire to eliminate fear.)

Like third party conversations, sarcasm is cowardly when used with adults and when used upon children it can be absolutely cruel and abusive. Even when used "good-naturedly" (as in kidding,) sarcasm often has a cost - the avoidance of intimacy. It is often used as a way to "be" with someone we like, when we fear a more genuinely intimate way of interacting. Sarcasm is a very prevalent way of speaking among pre-adolescents, adolescents and teens. Men more than women, resort to kidding or wit as a way of fostering relationships as well. In most of these situations, however, hidden under the kidding is a request for intimacy that sounds somewhat like this:

> *"Don, I really like you and you are fun to be with, yet I often don't know how to be in conversation with you, so I resort to "kidding". If I can "kid" with you and get you to laugh, then I get reassurance that you like me. I am afraid to trust you with some of my conversations that reveal who I am, because I am afraid that I might lose you as a friend. Since I like you, I am not willing to run that risk at this time, and therefore choose wit over intimacy. The truth is that I wish we could find other ways of acknowledging that we respect each other besides this constant game of seeing who can come up with the best pun, put down or play on words.*

Although sarcasm and biting humor can be a barrier to intimacy, wholesome laughter and lighthearted joking, can help to establish a bond of intimacy in our relationships with our family and friends.

Laughter is both good preventative medicine and curative medicine for what may already ail us. A family, class room, work place or social setting that encourages harmless, healthy laughter is usually a very uplifting environment in which to be. *In You Can't Afford The Luxury of a Negative Thought*, authors John Roger and Peter McWilliams have written a chapter entitled, **If It'll be Funny Later, It's Funny Now**. The premise of this chapter is that we often take our mishaps too seriously. We get stuck in the "little picture" difficulties in our lives when we could easily step back and in the big picture of life, enjoy our comedy of errors. The author, John Roger illustrates this point with the following passage:

Once I was traveling to give a lecture. The plane was late, and everyone else's luggage came off before ours. Somewhere across town, there were several hundred people in a rented hall waiting for me to give a talk - perhaps on the importance of being on time - and it was getting later and later.

Finally our luggage started to arrive. One suitcase had sprung open, and clothes were spread all over the conveyer belt. Another piece of luggage was obviously damaged. The people traveling with me were getting more and more upset. Finally I said, "Relax, this is funny. In a few weeks we'll be telling stories about tonight and laughing about it. If it'll be funny then, it's funny now." And we started looking at the situation as if it were a Woody Allen movie. When some of the luggage didn't arrive, we smiled. When the car rental company didn't have our reservation (or cars), we laughed. When we heard there was a taxi strike, we howled. Sure, everyone thought we were crazy, but we were having a wonderful time. When we finally got to the lecture, I had a great opening monologue.[24]

[24]John Roger and Peter McWilliams, <u>You Can't Afford The Luxury of a Negative Thought</u> (Los Angeles: Prelude Press, 1991), pp. 277-288.

The authors also emphasize, and I agree, that it is certainly not healthy to use laughter as a form of denial, or a way of avoiding the discomfort of necessary confrontation. Often however, the only difference between laughing about something and crying about it is the mood in which we choose to interpret the situation.

We all know that in parenthood, teaching, counseling, ministering and any vocation, there is ample opportunity to turn adversity into humor. Sometimes we simply need to stop and think of how funny it really is when our child has just used the bottle of hair color on the cat, or when we find our neighbor's two-year-old has poured our entire five pound bag of flour down the bathroom bowl. In the words of the authors above, if it will be funny enough to talk about tomorrow, then it's funny enough to laugh about today.

Like humor, inappropriate laughter can also be harmful to a child. I have all too frequently witnessed insensitive adult laughter inadvertently hurt a child. One example that comes to mind occurred at my daughter's dance recital. As a precious troupe of girls pranced onto stage and began to dance, one little four-year-old lost her tutu. Apparently it did not fit well and as she tried to pull it back up again, it kept sliding down to her feet. This maneuver had the audience in an uproar of laughter. Though I must admit it was funny to watch, this situation was clearly not a laughing matter to the child. The child was so embarrassed by the laughter that she took her tutu and ran off stage. When the audience realized their insensitivity, they all said Ohhhhhhhhh....Unfortunately, it was too little, too late. The damage had been done, and could have easily been avoided, had the adults in the audience thought before they began their laughter.

There are many other instances even worse than this where children have been the brunt of bad jokes. I have seen adults laugh at children when they say a word incorrectly or when they have tripped and fallen. Children do lots of things that seem humorous, but we should be cautious as to how we respond. We must be sensitive to how children might react to our laughter, and ask ourselves, "How would I have felt if someone laughed at me in the same situation, at the same age?"

Now it is important to teach our children how to laugh at their mistakes, but we don't want to risk offending them with insensitive laughter of our own. The best way I know how to teach my children to laugh at some of their innocent mistakes is to continue to laugh at my own. When I do laugh with them about theirs, I let them take the lead and I follow. It really isn't hard to judge when laughter is appropriate and when it is not. Just stay tuned into your child's feelings, concerns and requests, and I'm sure your laughter will be used to inspire joy.

With these words of caution, please laugh out loud and laugh often with the children around you. It doesn't take much to get a child into a belly roar, and it's fun for all who experience it. One of the greatest legacies we can leave our children is our laughter and sense of humor. When they watch us enjoy life and laugh a lot, they learn that joy and laughter are simple but profound ways of celebrating life, and that life itself is a privilege and a treasure. Laughter also releases chemicals in the brain that elevate our moods and which scientists have discovered aid in the recovery of illness.

It is very easy to find humor in our every-day lives without resorting to ridicule or sarcasm. Again, the life of a parent or teacher is filled with opportunities to enjoy laughter with children. We just need to assure that our humor is not a way of avoiding a deeper relationship with those we love, or used to express our anger in a covert way.

In summary, whether humorously or seriously spoken, many of our words pass undetected through the conscious mind into the deeper levels of consciousness where information is processed and stored. It is therefore, imperative to listen carefully to what we are speaking to our children, and it is best to keep conversations positive and direct. At those times when we do choose to use humor or indirect suggestions (as I discussed in the preceding section) we should do so with care.

Exercise 27

Instructions: If needed please review the descriptions of the types of suggestions that are discussed in this chapter and give examples for the following types of specific suggestions. It could be most beneficial if you used authentic words you have spoken in real situations with your children.

1. A negative suggestion with an implied meaning (See *Implied Indirect Suggestion*) _____

   _____

   _____

   _____

   _____

2. A negative suggestion disguised as sarcasm or humor (see *Teasing, Sarcasm & Humor*)_____

   _____

   _____

   _____

   _____

3. A negative suggestion in the form of teasing (see *Teasing, Sarcasm & Humor)*_____

   _____

   _____

_____

_____

4. An indirect positive suggestion given to your child (see _Indirect Verbal Suggestion_)_____

_____

_____

_____

_____

5. A positive suggestion spoken in front of your child to someone else (_see Indirect Verbal Suggestion._)_____

_____

_____

_____

_____

6. An alternative suggestion to your child (see _Alternative Suggestions_)_____

_____

_____

_____

_____

I hope this exercise supports you in becoming a very good observer of the way you give suggestions to your children and the other important people around you. I also hope it brings you to a heightened awareness of how other individuals make requests and give suggestions to you.

Though we need to take care with what we speak, it is not my intent in writing this book that you become overly vigilant or overly concerned about every word you speak or every word spoken to you. It would be counterproductive to the ease and flow of communication and would inhibit the spontaneity of playful conversation. This book was written with the intention of assisting you in obtaining the skills which will enable you to automatically speak to your children in empowering ways. In simply reading this book, the number of inadvertently negative suggestions, statements and requests will drastically diminish from your conversations, and you will notice that the number of positive ones, (conscious and unconscious, direct and indirect), will significantly increase.

If speaking in affirmative ways is difficult for you right now, I assure you, it will become easier with time and practice. Before long, the awkwardness or difficulty of changing the way you think and speak will diminish. When this occurs, speaking in affirmative, loving and empowering ways will become second nature to you and to those children in your life whom you cherish and love.

Refrigerator Post-it

Types of Suggestions

1. **Indirect verbal suggestion**: *It's cold in here.* (when we want someone to lower the air.)

2. **Passive Aggressive Suggestion**: *Is that the best you can do with your hair.*

3. **Third Party Conversation** (positive and negative): *Patrick looks handsome.*

4. **Implied/Indirect Suggestion** (positive and negative): *I bet you're proud of your hit?*

5. **Teasing**: *Look at you/him, crying like a little baby.*

6. **Sarcasm**: *I suppose it would be too much to ask for you to clean up around here?*

7. **Biting Humor:** *Sure she's smart if you compare her IQ to a chimpanzees.* (said with a hidden agenda to hurt her).

8. **Loving Humor:** *You're as cute as a bug's ear.* (said lovingly and affectionately).

*Children thrive most on
the free things in life -
your gentle touch,
your warm smile,
and your loving embrace.
Be generous with these.*

      anonymous

Chapter 13

Non-Verbal Conversation

(Body Language, Gesture, Tone and Manner)

Recently while in the park with Matt and Claire, I witnessed two mothers, in similar situations, communicate very different messages to their children - Both used words but spoke most clearly and profoundly through their body language and mannerisms.

The first mother that I observed was sitting thoughtfully on a park bench reading a magazine when she looked up in dismay to find her three-year-old child frolicking in a puddle of mud near by. Quickly rising to her feet she shouted, "Justin come over here right now!" Perhaps Justin was a bit too far away from his mother to detect the anger and disapproval in her voice, for he came running with a big happy grin, and his muddy little arms and hands outstretched toward her. As Justin came within a foot or so of his mother, she backed away with a quick jerk and with a stern look of disapproval exclaimed, "Stay away from me you filthy kid." I remember the look of confusion and then sadness on three-year-old Justin's face. From where Justin stood, his mother had called him to her, but when he eagerly responded and went to embrace her, she refused his embrace with body language and words that spoke rejection.

Like a blessing sent down from heaven, my attention was diverted to the second mother who had just discovered her own child playing with Justin in the same mud puddle. This time, the child's mother looked up and laughed as she watched her three or four-year-old having fun in the mud.

After secretly enjoying the scene for a moment or two, she calmly walked over to her son and said in a firm but loving tone, "I see you have found a mud puddle. I know mud puddles are fun, and those are your good clothes. So we'll have to go home now and clean those good clothes off." This mother then rustled her son's hair in a playful manner, smiled, and took his hand, gently escorting him to the car. I was clear that the boy understood that having to leave the park early was a consequence of playing in the mud puddle with good clothes, but I was also clear that he knew his mother still loved and approved of him as a person.

In Justin's situation his mother's concerns, which she expressed through her body and words, smacked passionately of anger and disapproval. In the other child's situation, the mother's concerns were also expressed through actions and words, but were clearly accepting and understanding of her child's nature. Here we had two very similar situations, two very different reactions from the mothers and, no doubt, two very different interpretations of the situation from the boys. The second situation was a poignant affirmation of understanding and acceptance from a mother to her child. Justin's situation, on the other hand, was one of rejection and disapproval not only for the trip to the mud puddle but for Justin himself. Justin's mother showed as clear a lack of empathy for Justin as the second mother displayed understanding and compassion, and from where I was sitting most of this communication occurred on a non-verbal level.

Mannerisms, gestures, attitudes, and all of the other actions which we generally designate as "body language" are very powerful suggestive tools in rearing children. Behavioral scientists speculate that our facial and body gestures and our tone of voice may account for as much as seventy five percent of what we are communicating.

As a counselor, I have been trained to listen attentively not only to words, but to eye movement, facial expressions, body gestures and body positions (arms and legs, posture, hand placement, etc.) and have been trained to listen for inflection and tone of voice as well. I do this because much is revealed through the more subtle communication spoken through the body. Young children listen attentively to body language as well. The following is a list of three reasons why in light of this fact, your non-verbal communications with your children are as important as what you speak out loud.

Why Body Language and Movement is Important

1. During the period of time when an infant and young child is unskilled at language, he relies on your touch, your tone of voice, your posture and your movements to assure him that all is well. He relies on these non-verbal gestures to develop a sense of the world around him, and a sense about your feelings toward him. An infant, for example, whose parents pick him up and comfort him when he cries, learns at a very early age that the world is a safe place in which to live. When he feels hunger, pain or fear, his parents are there to provide love and comfort. The non-verbal actions of being held and comforted encourage the first and most powerful seeds of security to grow within him.

2. Children rely on our non-verbal communication to help them understand our conversations and requests. Often as adults we have been conditioned to filter out non-verbal communicative gestures and listen only for concrete verbal content. One of the reasons we are conditioned to filter out non-verbal communication is because many of us have grown up in homes where our parent's gestures and tone contradicted what they were verbally speaking. For example, a parent might be yelling at a child, and in response the child asks the parent, "Why are you so angry?" The parent in turn, and in a very angry tone, declares, "WHAT ARE YOU TALKING ABOUT? I'M NOT ANGRY!" The child, trusting that his all knowing parent is correct, feels confused then begins to doubt his own ability to read others. His internal conversation may sound somewhat as follows: *My parent looks angry and sounds angry, but she says she isn't, so I guess I'm wrong again.*

Over time, the child learns to mistrust his interpretation of other's moods and learned to block out contradicting non-verbal suggestions in favor of spoken ones. Since very young children have not yet learned this art of selective perception, they still listen to our non-verbal suggestions as well as our words. The best way to help them grow to read body language correctly, be honest with us in return, and trust their instincts about others, is to keep our body language consistent with our verbal messages. In other words, we must all strive to be honest about what we are feeling and our children will have permission to do the same.

3. Affectionate touch as a form of communication is vital to a child's healthy physical growth and emotional development. Affectionate touch is absolutely essential for healthy physical and mental growth, not just in children but for all of us. Frequent physical displays of affection given by a parent to a child are very nurturing to the developing child's self-esteem and can literally help them to grow.

There has been an impressive amount of research done over the last century with respect to the importance of loving touch. Earlier in this century there were two classic and well known studies which linked touch to the mental and physical health of infants. One study was conducted in a World War II orphanage where it was found that physically healthy infants who were not frequently touched were much more likely to die within the first year of life than were healthy infants who were touched with regularity. In fact, there is a special designation for infants who die from lack of touch. It is called "failure to thrive."

The other study was done on primates. This study documented the mental and physical deterioration of newborn infant primates whose physical needs were cared for but who were deprived of physical contact with their mothers. Over time, these infant primates became profoundly anti-social and some became psychopathological.

Later in this century a very important study was done on premature infants. Back in the middle part of this century, pre-mature infants were thought to have a better chance of survival if handled only when medical treatment was needed. However it was shown that the pre-mature infants in the study who were frequently held and stroked by their parents and by the medical staff had significantly better prognosis than those pre-mature infants who were given the standard "hands off" treatment. Though this study transformed pre-mature infant care, it was not until recently when scientist discovered the physiological reasons for the touch related pre-mature, orphan, and primate health changes.

Dr. Deepak Chopra, world renowned endocrinologist and spokesman for mind/body health has devoted much of his life to the study of mind/body medicine and touch induced healing. In his studies he has found that when an individual is stroked gently on the skin, life enhancing chemicals, or neuropeptides, are released within the body. Most of us know what endorphins can do to elevate our mental attitudes, but endorphins can also help promote physical health and growth by elevating the levels of disease fighting immune cells, (such as T-cells, B-cells and macrophage,) and by encouraging growth hormones to work efficiently.

In Western medicine, these and other recent findings have opened up whole new areas of science, such as psycho-neuro-immunology, (the study of the relationship between one's psychology, neurology and immunology,) and have recently brought about the Federal Department of Alternative Medicine. Although Middle and Far Eastern medicine have used healing touch methods for centuries, Europe and the US are bridging the gap quite rapidly. Many nurses and physical therapists are attending seminars and classes for "healing touch." And healing touch is being used now in many main stream medical facilities to promote health and wellness for sick individuals, and to promote continued health and growth in healthy individuals.

The Importance of a Hug

Although there are valid scientific reasons to affectionately touch those we love, the simple truth is that, appropriately touching people we love feels wonderful, too. It gives us a sense of peace, security and a feeling of being cherished. It is one of the quickest ways I personally know how to enhance my own moods. In my family, we hug each other all the time. We rarely forget to hug each other good morning, hello in the afternoon, and goodnight at bedtime. We give lots of hugs for moral support, and my children will often offer me hugs when I am feeling stressed or tired. Nothing warms my heart more than when one of my children says, "Mom you look like you need a hug." I never refuse them either. Probably because it always manages to make me feel better.

I know many individuals who have found it awkward and difficult to hug others -- even their own husband, wife or children. When I have the privilege of counseling these individuals, I encourage them to take the plunge and begin to hug those with whom they have the most significant bonds. I advise them as I would any of you who find it difficult to show physical affection, to begin with small, soft quick ones. If the recipient is stunned or simply refused to respond with a reciprocal embrace, find someone who does, but don't give up on the others. With few exceptions, they will eventually come around.

If you continue to forge forth in this effort for loving physical contact, you will soon discover the many people who are lined up to receive your affection. We all need to be physically loved, and hugging is a wonderful way to care for ourselves and the other precious individuals in our lives.

Once you get the hang of it, you may enjoy hugging so much that you begin to hug people outside of your immediate circle of intimates. I often turn my back on traditional counseling protocol and hug my clients when they enter my office and when they leave. In counseling sessions I offer many hugs of moral support, and I have never had one client take this as a personal affront or as sexual misconduct. I have, however, had many grateful clients tell me how good it feels to be hugged with compassion, and how long it's been since anyone touched them in a caring way.

Remember the bumper sticker "HAVE YOU HUGGED YOUR CHILDREN TODAY." This slogan was used to promote family unity and healthy child rearing practices. Children, whether your own, a student of yours, your patient's, or a friend's, thrive and flourish upon hugs and other appropriate forms of physical affection. They are usually very eager to reciprocate and rarely reject the offer. Again, if your children are not accustomed to displays of physical affection by you, it may take a little while for them to come around. With persistence they will eventually bless you with spontaneous, loving hugs as well.

John Buscaglia, who is perhaps the world most preeminent hug and touch expert, has many good books out on the art and therapeutic value of hugging. If you presently have a difficult time showing physical affection, I recommend you read one of his excellent works. These books will convince you that healthy physical displays of affection are not just a luxury but are a necessity for the development of healthy children and for the continued development of healthy adults as well.

After you read this section, treat yourself to a wonderful pleasure. The next time you are in contact with your child (or any family member or friend) hug them, but to make it even more enjoyable tell them what you are going to do first. Let them know that you need a nice long hug (not to be mistaken with a quick burp-like pat on the back, or a half-hearted right shoulder to left shoulder squeeze.) Request that they hug you back. Allow yourself to really feel the sensations of the hug. Give the hug and the feelings that go with it your undivided attention - then observe the transformational experience that occurs.

Often when giving or receiving a hug from my husband, my children or a friend, it seems as though I just collapse into the feeling of it. The more I need the hug, the more comfort I receive from it. It is a wonderful gift that costs us all nothing to give or receive. A hug suggests to the individuals receiving them, you are special and I like to be close to you. We honor people when we allow them to touch us. It is a non-verbal message that tells another individual that they are valuable and lovable for who they are.

I also recommend that you establish a daily ritual of hugs in the morning, upon returning home from school or work in the afternoon, and before bed in the evening. You will be astonished at how often these hugs set the tone for your family's day, remainder of the evening or peaceful rest at night. And while your hugging, an *I LOVE YOU or YOU ARE SO SPECIAL TO ME* works wonders too!

Non-Verbal, Non-Physical Affection

Hugs, kisses, pats, strokes or any form of healthy, relationship appropriate physical affection is an excellent way to enhance our home, classroom, or work environments. Affectionate, non-verbal communication comes in non-physical forms as well, and can at times be just as uplifting as a kiss or hug. A well placed wink, thumbs up or a thoughtful and considerate laugh or smile for example, can also be powerful non-verbal tools of suggestion.

Recently while listening to a lovely young lady play the violin at a church service, I witnessed her mother perform a very simple gesture that packed a powerful message. Though the young lady's performance was lovely, it was not without obvious flaw, and after finishing her piece, I could tell by the girl's embarrassed facial expression that she knew this as well.

It just so happened that I was seated behind her mother, and when she looked to her mother for validation, her mother gave it to her. Her mother smiled brightly and proudly and with a thumbs up sign, the girl's face began to beam. It was a touching moment that I shall remember for a long time. The simple gestures of a smile and a thumbs up shifted the violinist's mood and turned a situation that could have left the girl disheartened, into a situation that gave her a sense of pride and pleasure for her performance.

Warm smiles, winks and waves are all ways in which adults can express approval, kinship, warmth and love. Children need those affirming gestures to develop a strong and healthy self-image and as encouragement to face the world with a healthy attitude. Genuine smiles convey an especially warm and loving message when they are in response to a child's actions. Like the "it's all right" smile that occurs when a child has accidentally spilled his drink at the dinner table. This type of positive reinforcement, strengthens the belief that it's acceptable to be human and make mistakes.

One of those perfect moments of parenthood that I spoke of earlier occurred some time ago when my son accidentally broke a very special porcelain vase of mine which had great sentimental value and had been given to me as a wedding present by a dear old friend. Matthew had been helping me dust the furniture, when I heard a thump and heard him gasp. As I turned to look at him, I saw my vase sway back and forth on top of the table and then come crashing down into several pieces. I then saw the look of fear in his face, and as the tears welled up in his eyes, I quickly moved across the room toward him. When I reached him, I immediately gave him a big hug. I then assured him that I was sad too, but that accidents happen to all of us. I also told him how frightening it is for me to accidentally break something that belongs to someone else and how I sensed that he must be feeling pretty much the same.

The payoff for my understanding came when he gently pulled away from my embrace, took my face in his little hands, and with tears in his eyes said; "Mommy I love you very much." At that moment I could sense exactly what he was feeling. I knew he was overwhelmingly relieved, because I recognized that he had made a mistake, that he was frightened by it and that I chose to comfort him instead of yelling. This experience has had a lasting effect on both of us. I am still touched when I recall that situation. More importantly, when I do get upset that he or Claire have broken or spilt something that creates a mess, I remember that I have at times displayed love and acceptance in similar situations and could choose to react that way again if I come from a place of understanding.

For the sake of the children around you, be generous with your reassuring actions of forgiveness and understanding. Accidents and mistakes are necessary for growth. Mistakes are one of the most profound ways in which we learn. In his early attempts to create the light bulb, Thomas Edison was asked by a reporter how it felt to fail over a hundred times at inventing a light bulb that worked. Mr. Edison, confidently and with dignity replied, "I have not failed one hundred times at creating the light bulb. I have learned over one hundred ways NOT to make a light bulb....". His healthy attitude about failure was part of the master recipe for Mr. Edison's unsurpassed ability to invent that which others could not even conceive. When we assure children that it's all right to make mistakes, we provide them with a safe space to be creative and innovative. They grow up being healthy risk takers, for they know that with every risk is an opportunity to experience and to learn something new.

Exercise 28

In response to each mistake below, list one non-verbal way in which you can reassure and support your child.

1. He's just spilled his milk onto the kitchen rug. _____
   _____
   _____

2. She struck out with bases loaded, one point behind, at the bottom of the ninth. _____
   _____
   _____

3. Your sixteen-year-old drove the car into the garage door while the door was still closed. _____
   _____
   _____

4. Your child has just been criticized by his peers and feels sad and embarrassed. _____
   _____
   _____

Though I prefer to stay within the realm of "what to do" with children, I think that the following list of non-verbal things to avoid is essential to our ability to gesture and move in a way that promotes our children's healthy growth and success. So here is a small list of non-verbal suggestions that you want to "remember to forget."

A List of Things to Forget

1. Finger Pointing - Remember when you were told that it was impolite to point at someone? Well it still is, and that goes for pointing at a child too! Pointing a scolding finger at a child is a sure way to inhibit open, effective communication. The finger, especially the index and the middle ones, serve to distance us from the true meaning of what the finger pointing individual is really trying to communicate. Pointing an accusing finger at a child or adult is a lot like those "You make me so mad when you...." statements. It elevates the finger pointer to a position of arrogant superiority, and puts the recipient in a defensive mood. The dance that both are doing in this situation becomes an impediment to healthy communication and a barrier to any peaceful resolution.

When verbally disciplining your child, I recommend that if they let you, you hold your child's hands in a loving way instead. This lets them know that even though you are upset or angry with their behavior, you still love and respect them.

2. Standing over your child with your hands on your hips - Imagine for a second how you would feel if someone close to seven feet tall like Michael Jordan, was standing over you with his hands on his hips, yelling or calling you down for something you did? I for one would be a pretty intimidated individual. That's how your children feel when you stand over them with an intimidating posture while you reprimand them for their mistakes. The suggestion or message they receive with this non-verbal form of communication is: "I'm much bigger than you, and I'll use force if I have to."

The bottom line is that you want your child to respect you and honor the requests you make of them, but it is very counter-productive for your child to fear you. Why? Because, many behavioral science experts and philosophers believe that fear and love are opposing emotions and cannot co-exist. I also believe that love and fear cannot be felt simultaneously. I know in my own spiritual development, once I stopped fearing God, as I had been taught to do in my religious training, I was able to truly develop a deep and meaningful relationship with him/her. I now see that there is a profound difference between fear and respect. I believe that we should honor and respect our parents and God, but we should not fear them. For fear is an impediment to the very development of love, respect and the appreciation we are striving to achieve.

We are also more highly motivated to succeed when we respect and love someone than when we fear them. Just think about this concept for a minute. Like me, sometime in your life, you have probably had both a boss that motivated you through intimidation and a boss that motivated you with positive reinforcement and a caring attitude. For which of those two individuals did you want to cooperate with most and perform your best? The same is true for children. They tend to be motivated most through loving, kind and respectful leadership.

I advocate that when communicating with your child, you make your size less formidable, by either lifting the child to your eye level, perhaps sitting them on a stool or cabinet, or better yet, by coming down to their eye level. I usually achieve this by kneeling when they are sitting or sitting down in a squatting position facing them squarely. Conversing with them from eye level allows them to feel respected and affords them the opportunity to listen more attentively as they look into your eyes. It also makes it easier for them to communicate appropriate feelings back to you as well.

3. Jaw and fist clenching, teeth gritting anger - My rule of thumb here is that if you feel angry enough to clinch your jaws or fist or grit your teeth, then you are too highly emotionally charged to be of any benefit to your children at that moment. If at all possible, remove yourself from the situation until you cool off. If need be, lock yourself in your room as I have on occasion, and only after you feel your jaws, teeth and/or fists completely relax and your mood relax as well, proceed with the discipline or discussion. There are few things that need such immediate attention that they must be addressed in a rageful mood. Remember any suggestions or comments coming through clenched teeth or jaws sends with it a message of hostility and resentment, and these emotions are an impediment to successful communication. Simply stated, resentment and rage are unhealthy moods in which to communicate. They are unhealthy moods period. Righteous anger and indignation, however, can be powerful moods from which to speak our concerns as long as we do so with respect for ourselves and the other person. I believe that if all communication occurred in a respectful manner, no matter what our mood, we would all be living in a peaceful and harmonious world. We parents have the power to make this global change occur by starting this practice in our own homes.

4. Corporal Punishment - Last but not least, I come to one of the most controversial subjects of this century. Few parenting manuals are written without this subject being addressed, and I am often asked as a parent and as a teacher whether I feel it is right or wrong to hit children. My answer is always clear and concise. Physical punishment is a highly ineffective form of behavioral shaping and quite often has detrimental effects on the person upon whom the punishment has been administered. It is also a violation of an individual's human and divine rights. When parents hit children, they erroneously assume a position of dominance and superiority, and they unknowingly strip the child of his dignity and honor.

I sometimes hear developmental experts make statements such as, "It's O.K. to spank your child as long as you do it when you are in complete control," or, "It's fine as long as the parent feels O.K. about doing it, and the child doesn't pick up on any guilt the parent may be feeling." I would like to state here that I respect the opinions of my colleagues, but I firmly and categorically disagree with their use of logic.

There have been scores of studies that have shown that corporal punishment is highly ineffective at producing positive behavioral change. There have been several other studies that have suggested that over 90% of all parents who use corporal punishment on their children often do so when they are frustrated, angry, or worse yet enraged. This indicates that parents often hit their children as an outlet for their own anger.

One of our country's most beloved and respected developmental experts, T. Berry Brazelton, MD, eloquently expressed my concerns and the concerns of many of my colleagues and friends when he wrote the following statement in an article written for April 1994's *Family Circle* magazine;

> *Don't spank or hit your child. Physical punishment conveys these messages: (1) Disrespect for the child; (2) I'm bigger than you, so I can get away with it; (3) Violence is the way to settle disputes. It also gives him tacit permission to behave violently. It's a well-known fact that a child who experiences violence reproduces it later on. Our society is already violent and abusive. Please don't contribute to that.*

I, too, believe that it is highly disrespectful to a child, and wounding to his developing personality and spirit to be physically assaulted in any fashion by an adult, and especially an adult whom he loves and looks to for example. The body is a sacred temple that houses the person and God's spirit inside. If we care enough about our children to shelter them from physical danger, and we care enough to supply their bodies with the nutrients they need to grow, then we should also respect their developing bodies by protecting them from acts of physical aggression - including those inflicted by us as parents. Remember their bodies and yours have to last a lifetime; teach your children to respect their bodies by respecting their bodies yourself. There are scores of other more positive disciplinary measures that can be used to guide children. I have outlined several of them in this book, and there are an abundance of other resources in which to find healthy behavioral shaping strategies.

If you are currently using physical forms of punishment with your children, I encourage you to consider some of the methods I have outlined, and read more on the subject of positive discipline. There is a small but profound book called *Without Spanking and Spoiling*[25] that I highly recommend as a supplement to this text. It outlines many positive disciplinary actions that can be taken in lieu of physically punitive measures. There are also many more helpful parenting books in print. Your librarian or bookstore attendant can assist you in finding books that will help you react to your children's disruptive or inappropriate behaviors with kind but firm measures and measures that will yield more positive and lasting results.

In summation of this chapter, I want to highlight some of the highly effective suggestions that we can give to our children to empower them to grow strong, healthy and happy. Children should be treasured more dearly and handled more carefully than the most rare and precious of gems, for they are worth infinitely more!

1. Strive to create a positive outlook about parenting, about your children, about yourself and about life that supports your children in developing positive attitudes of their own.

2. Show your children how special they really are by openly and frequently displaying physical affection and other non-verbal forms of affection to them, like lots of hugs, kisses, pats, snuggles, strokes, hand holding, smiles, laughter, and even tears of joy.

---

[25]Jerry Wyckoff, Ph.D., and Barbara C. Unell <u>Without Spanking or Spoiling</u> (New York: Simon and Schuster, 1984)

3. Demonstrate your non-verbal and non-physical approval with genuine smiles, winks, nods of approval, thumbs up, and loving eye contact.

4. Create an atmosphere of warmth, celebration, encouragement, and enthusiasm. In this environment, all children and adults can learn to grow healthy and happy. This means giving up the wining and self-pity to which many of us have grown accustomed.

5. Show your children how wonderful they are to be around simply by maintaining an attitude of thankfulness and appreciation for the precious gifts of life that God has bestowed upon us. If you genuinely hold your children as gifts and precious treasures, it will emanate out in your actions, gestures, looks, words, and in their glowing faces.

Exercise 29

Replace the following negative non-verbal disciplinary measures with positive non-verbal or verbal behavioral shaping measures.

1. Spanking your child for hitting her sister. _____

_____

_____

2. Tight liped, clinched jawed, disapproving stare when your child drags dirt into the house with his shoes. _____

_____

_____

3. Pointing a scolding finger in your child's face as you speak your disapproval of his own spoken anger. _____

    _____

    _____

Throughout the day, periodically do a mood check on yourself. Ask yourself whether the mood in which you are currently immersed is a mood from which you would like to be parented.

The *Refrigerator Post-it* on the following page is a mood scale you can keep on your bathroom mirror, desk, refrigerator or other obvious place. This will help you support yourself in remembering to check in with your mood and re-adjust it when needed.

Mood Chart

Empowering/Optimistic Moods

content, grateful, peaceful (easy going)

passionate, enthusiastic, energetic, excited

compassionate, accepting, forgiving, objective

actively loving (attentive to others needs and concerns)

creative, fun, enrolling

Non-Empowering/Pessimistic Moods

grave, solemn, sullen, resigned, depressed

crabby, bitchy, critical, judgmental,

nagging, petty, rigid, demanding

resentful, spiteful, vengeful, cynical

The parent who conveys his values
to the child as tidy principles,
and no more, accomplishes nothing.
Values appear to be best learned
from parents who do not only try
to preach them, but who also manifest
them in everyday interactions.

        Contemporary Perspectives

Chapter 14

Modeled
Communication
(Influencing Our Children by What We Do)

Frequently during my Master's and Ph.D work I wrote and spoke about my children's paternal grandparents and their parenting style as a living example of healthy child rearing. Abraham Maslow, one of the most preeminent psychologists and philosophers of the 20th century, devoted his life to the study of the mentally healthy or highly functional individual. I, too, find the study of healthy personality fascinating. In my observations of my husband and his parents and siblings, I have learned more about healthy development and healthy family than I have learned in any text book or course I have attended.

A highly functional individual is an individual who functions with confidence and without many ego defenses, who takes great care in the world around him, and who uses his talents and abilities and inner strength to reach for his full potential in life. The self-actualized individual often feels peaceful and joyful and feels a strong sense of accomplishment in many domains of existence.

It became evident very early in my relationship with my husband that he, his parents and his siblings were collectively and individually extremely well adjusted individuals. In an effort to further define what I mean by this, I will describe some of the characteristics that they embody.

1. They are mentally stable, high spirited individuals. (None of them have mental disabilities like neurosis or behavioral and personality disorders.)

2. They are ambitious individuals, successful in their careers and have college degrees ranging from Associates to Masters degrees.

3. They have healthy, close relationships with their parents, with their own children and with each of the nine other siblings.

4. They are objectively cheerful and optimistic in nature.

5. They are accepting of others.

6. They possess a high degree of honesty, integrity and moral behavior.

7. They are loving, charitable and kind in nature.

8. They are free from drug, alcohol or food addictions.

9. They have made significant contributions to the world around them by cumulatively raising 30+ healthy children of their own.

I know few other families that collectively possess all of these characteristics and function at this level. Considering there are ten children in this family, this a truly extraordinary accomplishment.

One of the profound bits of wisdom I have gained from observing my husband's family in action is that there were no extraordinary feats or abilities that helped create the nourishing atmosphere in which these individuals thrived. Frankly, their parents only displayed, what every parent SHOULD display to their children - warmth, acceptance, compassion, respect, trust and love. These are the major principles of this book.

I truly believe that we all have within the depths of our spirit the ability to extend this love, kindness, understanding, trust and respect to our children and to all living things. If you are a parent of children who are still living in your home, you will be amazed at how quickly they respond to and flourish upon the positive guidelines that I have outlined. Even adult children will eventually if not immediately respond to this kind of **unconditional** love, support and acceptance of who they are right now in their lives. (Remember also that acceptance of who someone is as a person is not the same as condoning all of their actions.) It is rarely too late to begin to develop a healthy relationship with your family. I have had the privilege of counseling many individuals, some with young children, others with adult children, who after applying the principles, underwent a major transformation in their parental/child relationships. If you are rigorous and committed, this will happen for you.

Blueprint For a Highly Functional Family

When I embarked on my quest to create an enriching and inspiring life for my own husband and children, I knew that I should explore the factors which made my husband's family of origin the successful family that they are today. I knew that raising ten healthy, happy, successful children was not a fluke of nature, but I was at first unsure of which of my in-law's many qualities had been the driving force behind the family's success.

I began by talking with several of my husband's siblings and with my husband himself. In all of these discussions I heard one resounding theme. Each sibling said that both of their parents consistently displayed or **modeled** the empowering behaviors that they grew up to possess and pass onto their own children. Knowing my mother and father-in-law as I do, this came as no surprise.

One of the qualities that I have found most profound about my mother-in-law, and one I seldom see as completely in others, is her lack of judgment, and consequently, her acceptance of other individuals around her. When a derogatory remark has been made in her presence about anyone, (her children, in-laws, friends or even a stranger) I have heard her consistently respond by saying something like, "Well we just need to allow them to be who they are, don't we?" or "We really don't know enough about what goes on inside their homes or their minds to pass judgment." Talk about take the wind out of the sails of gossip!

My in-laws are also very brave individuals, and came to the United States from Holland in 1956 with eight children and a few thousand dollars in my father-in-law's pocket. After immigration across the Atlantic on a ship, they made their home in up-state New York. There my in-laws bought a dairy farm which is now successfully owned by the eldest son. They also had their ninth and tenth children here.

I am told that the early years in New York were fairly lean. However, when I have asked my husband what it was like to live in a financially tight environment, he responded, "Hey, when you are a little boy growing up on a beautiful farm, all you need is a pair of jeans, a toy tractor and a mound of dirt to keep you happy. We never knew we had less than anyone else." Perhaps his perception is in part true, but I feel that his contentment with so little material wealth stemmed from the deep spiritual and emotional contentment felt within the members of his family.

My mother-in-law is also a delightfully warm and inviting person who possesses an unmistakable inner-peace. I have heard others share mother-in-law horror stories of meddling, criticism, disapproval and rejection. I feel very blessed, because I have always felt totally accepted and competent with her and have not once felt judged, been criticized or been given unsolicited advice. I notice that she treats her daughters, sons and other in-laws with the same respect. Years ago, I asked her how she resisted the urge to meddle in her children's affairs and I paraphrase what she replied: "*My mother once told me that my job was to build a warm and safe nest, and then to teach my children to fly, not to build a nest so secure and high that they would be imprisoned within it.*" Simple but profound wisdom!

My father-in-law also possesses the wisdom and behaviors I described above. With respect to running the family farm, he was fair and reasonable. I hear that he wasn't particularly generous with praise and verbal acknowledgment, but he did set clear expectations of them and acknowledged a job well done by giving them greater responsibility. He was strict and firm but motivated his children by helping them develop a sense of ownership for what they had. For example, when they were not in school, all five sons worked many hours tending the farm. My husband says no one really did much complaining though. When I asked him why no one complained, my husband replied, "Because, my father always made us feel that it was everyone's farm - kind of like employee owned businesses are today. My father instilled in us a sense of ownership and pride for everything we accomplished."

My husband John has also told me that his father instilled pride and ownership in their business, not only by soliciting their opinions and ideas, but by actually implementing a lot of their ideas as well. In part, John also attributes his self-confidence and self-esteem to his father's willingness to allow them to do anything they thought they were capable of doing. He states, "My father always assumed we could do something unless we proved otherwise."

Consequently, John was responsible for raising calves at six, successfully driving tractors at nine and undertaking any adult chore at fourteen. For some parents this might be too risky a chance to take with their children. For my husband and his siblings, the chance my father-in-law took at giving them major responsibilities, yielded impressive results. In my opinion, it was a risk well taken. I have seen the tragic decline that occurs to an overprotected child's self-confidence, curiosity and sense of wonder when a parent keeps the reins too tight. Despite some, great discomfort on my part, I tend to follow my father-in-law's example and give my own children greater responsibilities than many other children have at their age.

When one of my friends observed Claire, then six, cut her fruit with a sharp knife, she became concerned and asked me, "Aren't you afraid that she will hurt herself?" I responded with the same words I must continue to repeat to myself often. I said; "Yes, I am afraid that she will cut herself, but not half as afraid as I am that she will grow up lacking confidence in her ability to do things well." My children are not perfect, but they are growing up with self-confidence in many domains. I attribute that in part to my in-laws ideals and willingness to give their own children responsibility.

It might be comforting to all of us mere mortals to know that my in-laws are mortal too. They and their children admit they made mistakes along the way. Hearing anecdotes of their trials and tribulations was very reassuring to me that a parent does not need to be perfect in order to be highly successful at parenting. However, I believe that the majority of time, my in-laws modeled behaviors that would encourage in their children, self-confidence, success, integrity, compassion, high moral and ethical standards and a commitment to seek excellence.

Lead the way

My goal in sharing this personal information about my family, is to support you in understanding the importance of modeling to your children the behaviors you want them to possess now and as they develop into adulthood.

In his recent work, *Compassionate Child Rearing*, Robert Firestone states:

> *More important than specific training or disciplinary measures is the powerful effect of modeling derived from the child's living day in and day out with his parents.*[26]

This quote is affirmed by the old adage: "Children do as we do and not as we say."

---

[26] Robert Firestone, <u>Compassionate Child Rearing</u> (New York: Plenum Press, 1990)

I have heard parents joke by twisting that cliché in a tongue and cheek fashion saying, "Kids, do as I say and not as I do." At other times however, I have heard parents say it with conviction. They will smoke cigarettes or drink excessively for example, but shame and reproach their children for doing the same. Others will scold or punish children for lying, but expect them to lie and say that they are not home, when someone with whom they do not wish to speak, telephones.

I am not advising here that we allow children to lie, smoke or drink. What I am proposing instead may be personally challenging to many of us. I am asking that we model the behaviors, attitudes and ethics that nourish a whole, healthy and joyful existence. If we want our children to exhibit certain behaviors and attitudes, then we must exhibit them ourselves. If we don't want our children to exhibit certain behaviors and attitudes then we must assure that we don't model them with our own actions. I agree with Robert Firestone's suggestion. Modeling behaviors and characteristics, both life enhancing and harmful ones, is the most effective way to get a child to exhibit them himself.

Some years ago, there was a penetrating television commercial that stressed the influence of parental role modeling quite well. The commercial began with a father and his young son hiking in the forest on a beautiful day. As they hiked, the son followed closely behind emulating his father's every move. When the father decided to take a break and sit under a tree, the son sat down under the tree as well. When the father crossed his legs, the son crossed his. When the father scratched his head, the son scratched his. When the father took a cigarette from his pocket, and began to smoke it, the child picked up a stick and pretended to smoke it too. I don't think that the commercial had any words, and it certainly didn't need them. The impact from this non-verbal suggestion was very powerful. It was a dramatic illustration of how children look to those they love for guidance.

It is the nature of almost all animals, including humans, to emulate without question, those who nurture them. Almost all species learn through example. Most of it is also done on a deeply subconscious level. Instinctive behaviors for example, have their roots in subconscious programming of past behavior. In order to preserve the survival of the species, observations of successful species behaviors are recorded and embedded in the subconscious mind of young animals and are then passed on from generation to generation through what scientists now refer to as "Cell Memory."

In this matter, humans differ slightly from other animals. The subconscious mind of the human often records and stores unsuccessful behaviors too. What sometimes occurs is what we often see today - a fair amount of life inhibiting behavior which is displayed simply because it was indiscriminately recorded into the subconscious mind. This makes it all the more important to model highly effective and functional behaviors to our children.

As adults, we can erase life inhibiting subconscious recordings by replacing them life affirming ones. The more we exhibit the more effective behaviors, the greater our chances of extinguishing the undesirable ones.

I would also like to stress that teachers, day care providers, counselors, ministers and anyone else who is influential in a child's life, should be mindful of what you model. I have heard many personal accounts of individuals who have been profoundly influenced by the exemplary suggestions of a teacher, scout leader, counselor or other significant individual in their lives. When I was a teenager, I myself met a lady whose influence altered my life dramatically.

As a 10th grade student, I had no intentions of going to college. I had a steady boyfriend and, as was typical in my small home town, had every intention of marrying him when I got out of high school. In 11th grade however, I became fascinated with my high school counselor, who I assessed as attractive, twenty-five, engaged, sophisticated and intelligent. I perceived her to be a near perfect example of a woman. By the end of that school year, my desire to imitate her life style had become so great, that I broke up with my friend, took my SAT test and sent my application to several colleges. The rest is history. I married at twenty-six, and now have my Ph.D in counseling psychology.

Though my choices to become a counselor and marry at twenty-six, were not consciously motivated by knowing my high school counselor, who knows, there just might have been some subconscious work at play. My life may have turned out quite differently had I not had such a strong desire back in 11th grade to imitate the behaviors and characteristics of my guidance counselor.

In Lee Salk's recent work titled *Familyhood*, he states:

> In my work in residential treatment settings and in my clinical work through the years, I have been most intrigued by those people who turned out better than, by all indications, they should have. Individuals who survived appallingly dysfunctional families, who navigated a path through terrible adversity and prevailed in the face of circumstances that predictably should have led them to jail or serious psychopathology. What happened? In almost every case someone significant and responsive was present in the individual's early life. Perhaps a grandmother, a social worker, a teacher who encouraged and praised and pushed the child to yield his best efforts or a neighbor who wasn't reluctant to intervene to fill the empty spaces.[27]

The message that I personally received from this passage and the one I would like to extend to you is that even if you are not a child's parent, if you have regular contact with a particular child, you can still have a profound influence on the child's quality of life.

---

[27] Ibid., p. 54.

Young children are especially influenced by their teachers and day care providers. I recommend that if you are a teacher, day care provider, counselor, minister or any other person responsible for the care of young minds, you develop a healthy respect for the power that has been bestowed upon you and the powerful influence you render by your example. If you are a parent, it would be wise to select day care providers and teachers, when possible, who display behaviors and characteristics that you will want your children to emulate.

Parents, teachers, counselors or any adult who has an influential position in a child's life, must take a sincere look at what you model to the children who are influenced by your actions, thoughts, words and mannerisms. You might begin this endeavor by writing a list of things that you want to see your child become and accomplish. Then examine whether you model these behaviors, traits and attributes yourself. Acknowledge and reward yourself for those things you are successful at modeling. For those important traits that you do not yet possess, devise ways to make them a part of your life today.

Even if you want more for your children than you have yet been able to accomplish for yourself, right now is the best time to begin accomplishing them. Becoming what you want your children to become is also the best way I know how to overcome the unhealthy desire to live through your children's accomplishments.

If for example, you want your children to get a college education and you have not done so yourself, consider obtaining your GED if you need to and/or take a college course. Higher institutions of learning are making it very easy for working parents to take courses, and many local high schools now offer evening college level classes for the working parent's convenience. If your children's education is truly important to you, even taking one class a semester or year will set the right example. If they see you taking those important steps, they will be encouraged to do so themselves. My children loved the idea that their thirty-something year-old mom was studying her school work, while they were studying theirs.

If you want your children to be assertive, ambitious, confident and caring, do you consistently display these qualities yourself? How is your relationship with your spouse (or significant other if you currently have one)? Are you both compassionate, loving, kind and deeply committed to each other's growth? Each other's goals, needs and ambitions? Do you foster each other's spiritual, emotional and physical health? If you answer "no" to any to any of the above questions, then you may want to take the actions necessary to create those things in your primary relationship. For if you don't, statistics show that your children will likely have similar relationships with their spouses. Statistics also suggest that females who watch their mothers being verbally or physically abused, often attract abusive mates. Males who watch their fathers abuse their mothers tend to chose mates that they can abuse. The reverse is true as well.

Lead the way by positive example, and the likelihood of your child achieving personal success and having fulfilling relationships in life will be great.

Exercise 28

What I want for my children in the domain of Love is:

_____

_____

_____

_____

What I model in this domain is:

_____

_____

_____

_____

What I want for my children in the domain of Community (How they take care of the world around them) is:

_____

_____

_____

_____

_____

What I model is:

_____

_____

_____

_____

What I want for my children in the domain of Family is:

_____

_____

_____

_____

_____

What I model is:

_____

_____

_____

_____

_____

What I want for my children in the domain of Education is:

_____

_____

_____

_____

What I model is:

_____

_____

_____

_____

_____

What I want for my children in the domain of Dignity is (How we allow others to treat us and how we treat ourselves):

_____

_____

_____

_____

_____

What I model is:

_____

_____

_____

_____

_____

Refrigerator Post-it

- **My list of 10 behaviors and attributes that I want my children to possess, that I myself will practice and become more proficient.**

1.

2.

3.

4.

5.

6.

7.

8.

9.

10.

What Matters

*One hundred years from now,
it will not matter what kind of
car I drove, what kind of house I
lived in, how much I had in my bank
account, nor what my clothes looked
like. But the world may be a little
better because I was important in the
life of a child!*

author unknown

Chapter 15

What People Really
Want for Their Children

In the preceding chapters, I have set forth many distinctions about the power of language. I have discussed at length, the ways in which we can use verbal, non-verbal and modeled language to empower our children to develop in healthy and happy ways.

In chapter one, I provided a brief list of qualities that healthy individuals possess. Similarly, in this chapter, I will discuss many of the moods, behaviors and personality traits that the parents with whom I have consulted say they want their children to possess - Character traits which parents feel are most likely to create a successful, happy and health existence for their children.

This list of qualities I outline below is in no way complete, nor agreed upon by all parents. However, it can be used to assist you in developing your own list of parental priorities and objectives and may give you a clearer perspective on what it is that you are striving to achieve in rearing your children.

The group of parents that I consulted agreed that they want to instill in their children the following characteristics and qualities:

I. EMOTIONAL WELL-BEING

There are so very many aspects to emotional well being - ranging from the most profound ones like sanity to the more subtle ones like contentment and bliss. Basically the traits of emotional well-being that parents desire for their children are:

- self-confidence
- freedom from neurosis (ability to make grounded decisions and take mature actions)
- emotional balance
- happiness, contentment and peacefulness
- success
- freedom from addictions
- confidence in their interactions with others

Are these some of the traits you want your own child to possess? If so, the following recommendations are actions that you can take today toward supporting your children in their emotional growth.

A. Self-Confidence - Model self-confidence yourself through your words, deeds, attitudes and level of self-respect. Learn to unconditionally appreciate yourself for what you are truly worth. Each human being, whether black, red, white or yellow, president or skid row resident, CEO or welfare recipient, is worth equally the same, and worth infinitely more than the most priceless material riches on earth. No matter what you have done in the past or what you are presently striving to overcome, treat yourself as the priceless treasure that you really are. Remember to give and insist upon that same respect from others in your life. When you possess self-confidence, your children learn to become self-confident by emulating you.

If you feel that you need help in achieving a deep sense of self-esteem, you might consider individual therapy, a support group, and/or any of a number of excellent self-help books on the subject of personal success.

Remember that it is your birthright as a human being to create joy, love and happiness in your life. If your parents and other significant people in your life cannot provide you with the tools you need to have this inner success, now is the time to actively seek the support you need.

B. Freedom from Neurotic Tendencies - First take a close look at which, if any, irrational, life inhibiting beliefs or behaviors you possess. Which thoughts and actions of yours inhibit you from living life to its fullest? Do you have irrational fears or phobias? Are you a perfectionist whose perfectionism often prevents you from enjoying your life or your possessions? Do it cause problems in your relationships? Do your fears prevent you from partaking in life to its fullest, like a fear of flying, driving, heights, elevators impending physical harm or even more paralyzing - the fear of leaving your home? Any behavior that prevents an individual from expressing himself fully as a human being or inhibits him from interacting with the world around him in a productive way can be considered neurotic in nature.

Neurotic tendencies are rooted in irrational, ungrounded or poorly grounded beliefs. A woman, for example, who vacuums herself out of the house in the morning may have a poorly grounded belief that she will only be loved and respected by her family or society if she is the "perfect: housekeeper or wife or mother. A man who obsessively and compulsively washes his hands all day long, may have a poorly grounded belief that if he does not continue to wash his hands, he will catch a life threatening disease. Although both of these situations may sound absurd to many of you, both are fairly common in our culture.

Neurotic behavior prevents us from living fully functional lives, because it inhibits our freedom to make healthy, rational choices. Even though we want our children to have the freedom to make healthy choices, we sometimes inadvertently sabotage these efforts through our actions, through our words and through our thoughts. Therefore, the best way to teach your child to feel safe and at the same time take risks that promote growth and learning is by learning to feel safe and taking risks yourself. For some, we need only to develop an awareness of our neurotic tendencies to begin to resolve them. For others whose fears, compulsions and obsessive behaviors are more severe, competent psychiatric counseling can do much to alleviate the source and consequences of paralyzing or life inhibiting fear.

The most ironic part about neurotic behavior and thoughts is that they often produce the very things we fear. We all know of insanely jealous individuals, who out of fear of losing their spouses, manage to drive the spouse away with pathologically jealous accusations and behaviors. Or the child who had such tremendous test anxiety, that despite diligent work and sound knowledge of the subject matter, proceeds out of stress to fail the test anyway. This is what we call self-fulfilling prophecy, and it occurs all the time with neurotic disorders. In part, it occurs because the subconscious mind would rather be right than be happy. Essentially, the subconscious finds a way to make its greatest fears come true.

We certainly want more for ourselves and our children than negative self-fulfilling prophecy, so I strongly encourage those of you who have life inhibiting behaviors to take action to effect a meaningful change in your life. You have many options - personal and family counseling, self-enhancement workshops and literature are but a few excellent resources that are available to us all.

C. **Emotional Balance** - Much of what I have already said applies here as well. We must also evaluate whether we have a healthy balance between, work, family, hobbies, social interest and spiritual endeavors. In our lives today, we are often like the child who when presented with a choice of several candy bars wants them all. We have so many options, much more than individuals had even two generations ago, that in order to keep balanced we need to learn to prioritize, pick and choose carefully and say NO. NO is such a small word, but often so hard to get out of our throat and off our tongue. Yet in order to maintain a well balanced and well adjusted existence in a very demanding world, we must say NO to those things which do not fit into our priorities and to say YES more often to those things that do. If you have a choice between going to your child's school performance, helping the local garden club plant shrubbery in your neighborhood or working late at the office again, I advocate that you choose which **feels** the most important to you. To understand what is most important to you, you might ask yourself the following question, *In twenty years, which of those three options above would I regret missing the most?*

Or you might ask yourself, *Which of these three options would give me the most peace and joy?* For me it's easy. My children are most important to me, and give me immense joy. I believe if I missed their performance in a school play, I might regret that decision in twenty years. My present career and the garden club may not even be a part of my life in ten years, so I don't believe I would live in regret for having missed those opportunities. For others of you this may not be as cut and dry a decision, nor am I suggesting that my decision and my priorities are right for everyone. What I am suggesting is that in order to achieve a healthy balance in a fast paced world, we must continue to assess which things are most important to us and make choices based on those priorities.

One important aspect of making decisions and keeping balance is our lives is our ability to say **NO** to those invitations or requests we want to decline. Often this is hard for adults. I have learned by examining my own reasons for over committing, that I often said YES to things I really wanted to say NO to, because I desperately wanted to be liked and approved of by others.

In an effort to seek love and approval from others, we fail to decline requests that do not serve in helping us maintain peace and balance in our lives. This often occurs because many of our parents did not give us the space to decline some of the requests they made of us. When we did decline, we were punished or ridiculed and sometimes made to feel unloved. When I began to realize that people still liked me when I learned to say NO and that they often admired me for my ability to do so, it became easier to assert my needs and set clear priorities. It has also become less important to me to win the approval and friendship of everyone I meet.

Those insights were truly liberating to me. There is a lot of value for you and your children too, in being able to confidently say NO. Like, "NO! I do not want to do drugs with you buddy." or "NO! I will not allow you to treat my body with disrespect."

If you want your children to have peace and balance, allow them the right to say **NO** sometimes. Children who are not occasionally allowed to say No to a request or who are not allowed to have a voice and vote that matters in their homes, are likely to grow up to be "YES" people as adults. I refer to "Yes" people as those of us who find it extremely difficult or sometimes impossible to say No to any request another person makes - Even to the ones above. Learning to say YES or NO when we want and need to, eliminates a tremendous amount of life stress.

Another link in the chain of personal balance and one that supports me in keeping my children and myself calm in the midst of our fast paced lives, is the elimination of such stress producing phrases as "HURRY UP, WE'RE GOING TO BE LATE," and "COME ON, MOVE IT OR YOU'LL BE LATE." Almost more than anything, I want my children to lead relaxed, calm and peaceful lives. It hit me like a bolt of lightning one day that every time I rushed my children or myself, verbally or non-verbally, I was driving a bigger and bigger wedge between them and their inner sense of calmness. I was inadvertently teaching them how to feel rushed, get frazzled and become stressed in their day to day existence.

Since receiving this insight, I have devised ways in which we can stay calm while doing such potentially stressful things as getting up and out of the house in the morning for school and work. One way I accomplished a sane and calm morning departure is to set a timer for the children (and myself) and put it in plain view. When the timer goes off the first time, they should be fully dressed. When I reset the timer and it goes off the second time then they must be finished eating and ready to get on their bikes for school. It works great, because they can hear the clock ticking and see the hand move slowly toward "0". We're rarely caught off guard and morning time is no longer plagued with "Type A" producing phrases such as, "Hurry ups" and "We're all gonna' be lates."

I also limit the amount of activities in which my children can partake. Both are allowed to choose two activities that they most want to pursue each season. I also solicit the efforts of other parents to car pool to practices. My decision to limit my children's extra-curricular activities came by way of observing other parents who felt it necessary to allow their children to partake in soccer, swimming, dance, karate and piano all at the same time.

I am clear that most of these harried parents, choose this lifestyle with their children, because they believe it will help establish a healthy balance in their children's lives. What often happens instead, is that both parent and child become so consumed by their hectic schedules that they have no balance to their lives at all. They are driven by the desire to partake in everything that life has to offer, and they forget that much of life's most precious moments are spent in solitary pleasure of their own and their family's company.

For your children to develop balance you must develop ways to eliminate unnecessary stress and activity in all of your lives, choose a select few activities that bring you the most joy, and discover ways to create peace, and creative quiet time in the pleasure of your own home environment.

D. Joy and Peacefulness - As was discussed in the section on Mood, a parent's level of contentment, joyfulness and happiness in life is fundamental to the child's ability to be happy, peaceful, joyful and contented as well. Feeling at peace with the world stems from achieving a deep level of inner peace for who we are and what we have been given in life. Our homes can and should be temples of peace and harmony for each individual living there. Again, the best ways I know to develop a profound level of happiness and peace with myself and with life is by focusing on all that I have been given in life, and honoring myself as a worthy and deserving human being of the things I have been given.

Living in gratitude affords me a tremendous sense of well-being and peacefulness. As I mentioned in the section on counting our blessings, one of the best ways I know to develop a profound level of happiness and peace with myself and with life is by focusing on my blessings. As I once heard Dr. Wayne Dyer say, *There is no way to peace, peace is the way.* I would also like to add that: Happiness does not come from outside of ourselves and bore its way in, but happiness must come from within ourselves and emanate out.

As a counselor, I have observed time and time again, that the easiest patients to support in making significant changes and the ones who make the greatest shifts in therapy, are most often the ones who have a deep sense of gratitude for what they have been given in life and for life itself. This level of gratitude is not measured by how much they have - For some of my clients have little and some have a lot. It is measured by how appreciative they are for what they do have. Loved ones, sunsets, food, shelter, educational opportunities, health, flowers and rain are some of the things almost all of us have to be thankful for, and these things, each and of themselves, are monumental qualities of life.

E. Success - About success, Ralph Waldo Emerson wrote:

To laugh often and much;
to win the respect of intelligent people
and affection of children;
to earn the appreciation of honest critics
and endure the betrayal of false friends;
to appreciate beauty, to find the best in others;
to leave the world better, whether by a healthy child,
a garden patch or a redeemed social condition;
to know even one life has breathed easier because you
have lived. This is to have succeeded.[28]

For me, his words are the essence of success - the essence of what I strive to achieve in my life. To live in gratitude, to have confidence in oneself, to laugh, to care for and appreciate others and to leave the world a better place are the true hallmarks of success.

Similarly, Lee Salk in *Familyhood* suggests, *that in order to feel successful, a child needs to feel that she can do something to the world and the world will respond.*[29] To foster this kind of personal success in children, we must first acknowledge the good things they do for others and how, in their own way, they contribute to the well-being of mankind. Through many personal examples, we must also show them ways in which we have successfully contributed to our family, to our friends, to our community and to the world around us. Keep in mind you do not need to be as altruistic as the late Mother Teresa to contribute and feel personal success. Profound personal success can occur every time you bend down to pick up a piece of trash in the park, or when you stop to help an elderly person load her groceries into her car. For your child, it can occur when he cleans his room, feeds the

---

[28]Ralph Waldo Emerson, Origin of Quote Unknown.

[29]Ibid., p. 76.

dog, or when he makes a pitcher of lemonade for his friends who are playing outside. My experiences have consistently shown me that there is no better way for me to establish healthy self-esteem than to feel that I contribute to the welfare of the world around me - As a friend of mine says, "To feel that I contribute in a way that pays my rent here on earth."

Most success in life also transpires through a mood of ambition (motivation, enthusiasm and perseverance). As I have stated throughout this text, the best way to foster ambition in your child is through you own mood of ambition and by consistently giving your child sincere acknowledgments and a lot of encouragement. Healthy ambition is hindered by ridicule, or through a parents' fearful unwillingness to delegate responsibilities to their children (overprotective parenting). When I speak of overprotective parenting, I refer to parents who do not allow their child to partake in activities that the vast majority of other parents worldwide allow their children to partake in at any given age.

I know many people who I would personally and professionally assess as overprotective of their children. This form of neurotic behavior may show up as insisting their child wear a winter coat on a sixty degree day, or only allowing him to ride his bike in the cul-de-sac- at age ten while all other children in the neighborhood are allowed to ride their bikes down the street.

Overprotective parenting is often caused by an exaggerated fear that something bad will happen to one's child. The parent acts over-cautiously in an attempt to prevent anything bad from occurring. When confronted with their over-protective behavior, they often justify their actions by insisting that they care more about their child than others around them, or that their child is not as responsible as the other children of his age. What they don't see in the latter case is that their overprotective behavior usually results in a lack of mature behavior on the part of the child. In the former justification, what the parents fails to see is that one of the most loving and caring things we can do for a child is give her lots of person freedom so that she can become confident and capable.

I truly believe that these parents believe they overprotect out of a deep sense of caring. The more likely truth is that their desire to protect their child to this extreme is an unhealthy fear of loss. It is a crippling form of neurosis, both to the parent and child. It is all about the parent's fears and has little to do with the child's true needs. This behavior often takes care of the parent's fears at the expense of the child's need to have freedom, independence and engage in slightly risky age-appropriate activities such as roller-blading, hockey, diving, football, biking, etc. It is not a genuine act of love for the child.

Overprotective behavior on the part or the parent, greatly inhibits the developing individual's desire to explore his world and seek challenges. Since the overprotected child has been sheltered from risk, when faced with something that involves even mild risk, he may back away in fear. To be successful in life, an individual needs to have learned how to take risks, make mistakes and deal with the consequences. The overprotected child does not learn these skills.

Parents may also unintentionally sabotage their children's self-confidence and desire to succeed by requesting that their children accomplish a task then go directly back behind them and finish or re-do the task to the parent's satisfaction. Though this may not look like ridicule - IT IS. It is simply a more covert way of criticizing someone's efforts. There are times when I have been guilty of doing this myself. I would request that Matt and Claire help me set the table or polish the furniture, and after they declared the job complete, I would praise them for their effort as I proceeded to re-arrange the plates, or wipe the dust off the table. It became clear that they viewed the praise I gave them as very insincere and saw my need to go behind them and re-do as a declaration of a job poorly executed. What I have also discovered is even if I wait to return to the bedroom and re-make the bed behind them, they will notice it, and feel incompetent in their efforts to accomplish tasks successfully.

With respect to your children's accomplishments, there are several ways in which you can instill a sense of successful task completion that will motivate them to have the confidence to succeed in the future:

Setting Clear Standards of Satisfaction

First remember that an adult's standards of satisfaction are very different from a child's. I am clear now that when I asked Matt at four years of age to make his bed, his idea of a successful bed making mission looked very different than mine. To Matt, lifting the comforter over the bundled bed sheets and blanket looked neat and tidy. That's because a child of four neither possesses the physical dexterity nor the attention to detail to make a bed to an adult's standard of satisfaction.

Back then I didn't have the level of awareness that I do now that would have allowed him to feel successful in his bed making efforts. I would thank him for his attempt by saying "Good try," and at the same time, re-make the bed the way I wanted it to be make. Now that I am a little older and wiser, I often swallow my ego's fierce need to "look good," "be right," or "know more," and I allow Matt and Claire to do the best job they can and leave it at that. If the bed has lumps in it - So what. That won't stop the world from turning. If Claire decided to put the forks and spoons in the plate instead of on the napkin - It really doesn't hurt our digestion any. If Matt thinks his red and blue striped shirt looks good with his burgundy shorts - I can live with the assessment that his mother has poor taste if choosing his own clothing helps him develop a sense of accomplishment.

To be successful in life, children need to feel good about their accomplishments and they can only do that if we allow them a lot of freedom to feel that their best efforts are complete and satisfactory as they are. I highlight the term "best" because I am clear that I would also be undermining my children's healthy development if I were to allow them to do a half-baked job, simply because they preferred to be doing something else at the time. The trick is to know when your children are working diligently on their task and when they are trying to get away with substandard performance. Success is also encouraged through praise and acknowledgment of good efforts, not efforts that are only performed perfectly or without care or concern for the outcome. In lights of these facts, parents can do several things to foster a sense of successful task completion.

1. Allow your very young child to make his bed or perform other appropriate tasks to his standards of satisfaction without your interference, and as he gets older continue to coach him lovingly on how to perform that task or make his bed at a skill level appropriate for his age.

2. Clearly and patiently outline the standards that you want from your child. Show him through your example (your hands on coaching) how you would like the task to be done. As any good manager knows, clearly outlining standards of satisfaction that fit one's age and competency level is crucial to the assured success of a mission. It is especially important to clarify our standards of satisfaction if we feel the job we give them must be completed in a certain way.

If I want for example, my children to retrieve all of their dirty clothes to be laundered, I will specifically request that they look under their beds, on the floor of the closet and in their bathrooms for clothes that need laundering, and that I need them to have all of the clothes in the green basket in the laundry room within the next hour. If I fail to be specific about the time, the task is liable to be put off, and I will need to repeat myself. If I fail to be specific about where they should look, they are liable to only retrieve the clothing in plain view. If I fail to be specific about where to put them, they may throw the dirty clothing into the basket with the clean ones. Then they and I will be left feeling frustrated by the need for further work on the project. If this scenario is repeated frequently, it can leave them with a sense of incompetence which leads to a fear of failure - The greatest enemy to success.

In summary, when we:
1. give our children a good level of age appropriate responsibility that is helpful to others and themselves,
2. set reasonable standards of completion,
3. step back and allow them to handle their responsibilities with a minimal amount of interference, advice or criticism and
4. consistently remember to acknowledge them for their efforts - We water the seeds for success!

F. **Freedom from Addictions** - The two best ways to keep your children free from addictions to alcohol, food, tobacco, drugs, work, etc. is to:

1. **Remain or become free from them yourself.**

2. **Employ highly functional parenting skills like the ones set forth in this book. If you do, then**

**your child will never need addictions to numb
the psychological pain of rejection and low self-
worth or to feel emotionally alive.**

To put it in somewhat simplistic terms, many addictions result
from chronically suppressed emotions. The addictions people
develop are either outlets for or the expression of emotions
that were not allowed to surface when they were children.
Addictions are also used to numb the deep emotional pain of
rejection and feelings of worthlessness that often result from
many negative messages given to them over time. Addictions
can also occur through observation. Eating disorders and
cigarette smoking are two examples of how we can learn to
become addicted by watching someone else indulge in their
addictions. The good news is that addictions are not as
difficult to overcome as many experts and lay people would
like you to believe. If you have an addiction that could be a
threat to you and your family, there is much hope if you are
willing to take action. For there are many exciting and
transforming therapeutic modalities that offer healthy
alternatives to one's addictions, such as Alcoholic's
Anonymous, and many exciting educational forums for healthy
living in general such as; Education For Living Seminars,[30]
Rational Emotive Living and Gestalt Therapy to name a select
few. All of the above have been extremely successful for
many.

The second major category in which parents want to see
children thrive is in the area and development of:

II. SOCIAL SKILLS

We are our children's role models for their developing social
skills. How we interact with our children and the others

---

[30] Education For Living Seminars, 3113 Ryan Street, Suite 3, Lake Charles,
Louisiana 70601, 1(888) 335-7952

around us is how our children will respond to us and the world around them. Let us examine some of the various ways in which the ever-social human species interacts with others. We will also examine how we can support the developing child master the social skills needed to create happiness, success and harmony in his interaction with others. The social skills that most of us want our children to develop are:

A. **The Ability to Develop Intimate Relationships with Others** - Making others feel valuable, important and comfortable around you and at the same time feeling important and valuable to others is the key to developing intimate relationships and excellent social skills. When we recognize our own importance as a contributing member of society while recognizing the equal importance of others, we establish a healthy rapport and deep connection with the world around us.

One of the most profound ways in which we can develop an intimate and mature relationship with another human being is by consistently acknowledging others for their contributions to our lives. Through my own personal experiences, I have recently developed a much deeper sense of how important acknowledging and honoring other is in developing a healthy and lasting relationship and in building self-esteem.

We all need to be acknowledged for the good things that we contribute to our loved ones and to the world around us. I have come to learn that speaking my gratitude to my children, to my spouse and to all the other people in my life is a big part of the foundations by which my healthy, intimate relationships are built. Being appreciated by others is a profoundly uplifting experience, and the ability to genuinely express appreciation for others is among the greatest social and relationship skills we can develop.

When is the last time you remembered to thank you child for taking a telephone message for you or thank your spouse for making dinner, changing the oil in the car or changing a light bulb? When is the last time you thanked a co-worker or assistant or boss for helping you with some of your work related tasks, or thanked a friend for being there to listen to your concerns? If you haven't done these things in awhile, why not? Why not speak your appreciation for them today?

These are all ways in which people in our lives show us that they love us, and as social beings we establish a big part of our identity by the acknowledgments we get from others. A person can do nothing so small for us that a thank you would not be appropriate.

Just recently an elderly man in the grocery store stopped me, held my hand, and sincerely thanked me for simply smiling at him. He told me that it made his day. Until that moment, I had barely been aware that I had even performed that action, or that by doing something which comes so automatic to me could have such an effect on someone's day. His acknowledgment left me with a deep sense of peace and validation and with a reminder that both in big ways and in many small, I can be a continuous offer to others around me. Had he not stopped to thank me, I would have missed a very valuable experience. I am forever grateful that he did.

Exercise 31

In the space provided next to each person below, record an action that the individual listed took on your behalf, for which you are grateful and for which you are going to thank him or her in the course of this week.

Mother/ Father (living or not)   _____

Spouse/ Loved One   _____

Boss/Co-worker/Assistant   _____

Children (list one item for each)   _____

_____   _____

_____   _____

_____   _____

_____   _____

There are so many ways to make others feel valuable and important in our lives., and feeling valued and important to others creates greater levels of intimacy in our relationships. When we request assistance and advice from others we honor them as having value to us. When we support others in their time of need, we learn that we can be of great value ourselves.

I would like to extend a word of caution concerning our offers to assist others - Many individuals try to assist others by giving unsolicited advice. Giving advice is a way of feeling important and needed. The trouble occurs when we offer it without another individual's permission. It causes conflict and distance between the speaker and listener, because unsolicited advice often leaves an individual with a sense that you feel he is incompetent to handle his own issues. That is precisely why it is important that we refrain from giving advice unless we feel it is necessary, or we have been given permission to offer it.

Even in my professional role as a counselor, when I feel I have something to contribute to another person's well-being, I first ask their permission to speak it by saying: "May I offer you a suggestion that has worked well for me?" or "Are you open to discussing some possible ways in which you might deal with that situation differently?"

Though people infrequently turn down my offers, my asking permission to make an "offer" or advise them, relieves them from the pressure of taking the advice. I have also found that others are less likely to hear it as a challenge to their own competency than when someone offers advice by qualifying their statement with such phrases as: "You know what you need to do?" or "If I were you I'd...." These last two statements elevate the advice giver into a superior position and often leads the listener to feel somewhat inadequate. Advice given in this fashion can create a block to intimate conversation and to the intimacy of our relationships - Particularly our relationship with our children. Children are much more likely to consider what you have to offer them when they feel their competency, independence and their dignity are respected.

Speaking with sensitivity to other's needs and feelings is essential to intimate conversation. Speaking in ways that devalue others is intimacy's greatest barrier. Speaking honestly but respectfully, speaking and showing our continuous gratitude for others, offering assistance to others in their time of need and asking for assistance from others, are all excellent ways we have of developing lasting, intimate, mature relationships.

I often see and hear parents demand certain social behaviors from children that they do not themselves display. What they do not realize is how much more effective their actions are than are their words. I have observed many social behaviors in parents that contradict the behaviors they are striving to reinforce in their children. Let's take a look at a few of the more common behaviors or social skills that we see parents exhibit that contradict the social behaviors we are trying to instill in our children. It is my vision that once we see how we sabotage or contradict those behaviors we want to see our children develop, we will be motivated to design ways to reinforce these sound, healthy behaviors instead.

B. Eye Contact and Attentiveness to Others - Have you ever uttered the following request to a child: "Look at me in the eyes when I talk to you" only to be frustrated by the child's unwillingness to comply with your request? He will look at the floor, at the ceiling, at the buttons on his shirt or anywhere but straight into your eyes. I think through simply observing my own behavior, I know why this is so.

There have been times, many more than I wish to recall, when my children have spoken to me, but I have not stopped what I was doing to look them directly into their eyes and show genuine interest in what they were saying - a courtesy I always extend to my clients, and usually extend to friends, to strangers and to other individuals with whom I interact. I sometimes notice this very same lack of eye contact and lack of enthusiasm in most other parents that I observe as well.

Once I became aware of the inconsistent manner in which I established eye contact with my children as opposed to others, I vowed to mend my ways. I knew that if I wanted my children to look me and others into our eyes when we spoke, I would need to extend that same courtesy to them. I realize we cannot always look our children in the eye when they are speaking. Like when the stir fry is cooking while our seven year-old son is attempting to relay a story about who won the spelling bee in Mr. Harding's 5th grade class, or when you desperately need to use the bathroom while your child is elaborating at great length about the alleged bully in her class who broke little Anna's red crayon. In tough times like these, I try to look into my children's eyes, touch them on the hand and say, "What you have to say is important, and I want to give my undivided attention to what you have to say. However, I need you to wait one, or two or three minutes while I attend to this first."

Frankly the ability to **STOP, LOOK AND LISTEN** to our children when they are speaking is a challenging thing to master. Especially if we have children who talk a lot, or who are with us all day long. In all honesty, there are times when I knowingly fail to establish eye contact with my children when they are speaking. Like when I am engrossed in work or a good book or when I have something on my mind. Other times I am simply not aware that I am not listening or maintaining eye contact until they have either begun to shout what they are trying to relay, or have walked away in silent exasperation. At other times I notice what I'm doing earlier on in our interaction, and immediately show more attentiveness. Though my attention skills and eye contact are far from mastered, I continue to make strides with my own attentive behavior to teach my children the importance of eye contact and concentration when others are speaking.

There are also big personal payoffs for teaching attentiveness to your children. Your children will develop a greater sense of self-worth by observing how attentive you are to what they have to say. Your family will become more open and successful at communicating their needs when they know others are truly listening, and as the level of attention to others increases, the possibility of miscommunications between individuals will decrease. In essence, stop, look and listen when your children are speaking and they will stop, look and listen to you and others when you speak to them. Most importantly, the more you show enthusiasm and interest in what they are saying, the more they will feel good about who they are. Healthy intimate relationships are established through the genuine commitment to listen to and understand and care for the needs and concerns of others. We can only do this by listening carefully to what others are striving to speak to us.

C. **"Common" Courtesy** - I know many parents that demand that their children show respect to them, but show less respect to their children and to others. They may for example, demand that their children say please and thank you to them and others (which, as I've stated, is a very important social courtesy to extend) but fail at appropriate times, to say please and thank you to their children. I have noticed that in my own life when I began to consistently show courtesy and respect to my children by saying please and showing my gratitude by saying thank you, my husband and children began to show me much more consistent respect and speak their own gratitude more frequently. The triple bonus for being respectful and thankful is that:

1. Your children learn to establish these courtesies in their own social training,
2. It makes them feel respected and valuable, and
3. Makes your interactions and conversations with them much more peaceful and profitable.

Speaking in a respectful voice, refraining from yelling, nagging and name calling) is another common, yet uncommon courtesy that expresses concern and compassion for others. In order for our children to develop this social skill, parents must rigorously engage in respectful conversation with them. If parents continue to speak with disrespect to their children, their efforts to enforce courteous behavior will be greatly diminished.

D. Peaceful Resolutions to Conflict - Recently while shopping at Walmart, I witnessed an all too typical scene. There was a father strolling his two children in a cart, when all of a sudden the older child decided to slap, for reasons I was not privy, the younger child in the face. Of course the younger child bellowed a horrifying scream, and without a second's delay the father in turn slapped the older child in the face, while saying, "I told you never to hit anybody."

In a previous chapter, I made my position quite clear with respect to corporal punishment, so for me this situation was a flagrant example of how the older boy learned his aggressive behavior from his parent. By slapping the older boy for slapping his brother what did the father really hope to accomplish? What lesson was the boy taught here? I suspect that he was taught, through example, that it is acceptable to use force when you are angry or you want something.

Peaceful conflict resolution avoids the trap of teaching your children how to "fist fight" for what they want. Peaceful conflict resolution is the art of negotiating or making a request with dignity and honor while maintaining respect for others.

We are often most successful at peacefully resolving conflict when we stand gently but firmly in our own dignity while we make our requests and speak our concerns. The best way to teach our children peaceful conflict resolution is to resolve our own conflicts with them, with our spouses and with the world around us in the peaceful and respectful manners we have discussed within this text. One of my favorite quotes of all time was a poignant example of peaceful conflict resolution. In the movie, Ghandi, when Ghandi meets the British Prime

Minister to discuss the independence of the Indian people from British rule, Ghandi greets the Prime Minister with the following acknowledgment:

I hope that our adversarial political positions
do not prevent us from respecting each other as men.

According to the movie, Ghandi's greeting set the stage for a peaceful and productive conversation with an authority who had little to gain by entertaining the requests of Ghandi and the Indian people. I am clear that when we speak to each other as dignified men and women, and communicate in a way that affords each of us our honor - peace in our homes, in our communities and in our world is inevitable.

E. **Warmth and Compassion** - Warmth is being kind and genuinely loving to others. Compassion is the act of understanding someone else's situation or point of view. Warmth and compassion are qualities that are most effectively taught to children through the warmth and kindness shown to them at home by their parents. Parents who are consistently warm, loving and compassionate with their children, rear children who are warm, loving, kind and compassionate to themselves, to their parents and to others.

I realize that compassion is one of those ambiguous words that is easy to say ("Have a little compassion, will you.") but difficult to describe. I will attempt to define compassion here, by giving you examples of what compassion "looks like" to me.

Compassion occurs when a parent, instead of yelling at or spanking his two-year-old who is throwing a temper tantrum, comforts the child instead - For he realizes that the child is hungry or exhausted or overwhelmed in his current situation and is handling it the best way he can with the skills that he has at present.

Compassion is taking the time to stop at your five-year-old neighbor's lemonade stand, not because you are particularly thirsty, but because you remember what it was like to be a five-year-old eager to make a little money.

Compassion is loving your sister or brother despite the fact that they are arrogant or self-righteous, because you know that their arrogance is an ineffective attempt at asking for love and approval from others.

Compassion is loving and accepting yourself despite the fact that you, too, have made mistakes that caused pain for others. You forgive yourself and love yourself despite your human frailties because you realize that you, like your brother or sister, are also human and have done the best you could with the level of insight available to you.

While living in Houston, I had a neighbor who exemplified to her children the opposite of compassion. Paradoxically, the mother was very warm, friendly and kind to people around the neighborhood. She often brought vegetables and fruit from her garden to the neighbors, and she was always very eager to help us in time of need. We all really liked her very much. Unfortunately and as far as I could gather, she did not display these same courtesies to the members of her family.

She had three beautiful daughters, ranging from 5 to 12 years of age. However, it would not be a stretch to say that each of her three daughters terrorized the other children in the neighborhood. They were assessed by other members in our neighborhood as rude, critical, belittling bullies. These behaviors had the entire neighborhood baffled and at wits' end. I would frequently hear my neighbors say in frustration; "How could such a sweet lady be a parent to such awful girls. Poor woman she sure doesn't deserve it." I wholeheartedly agree that she, nor her daughters deserved such unhappiness, but as I took a closer look inside the family circle, I began to see what was happening to her and her daughters.

Though I am very cautious when I use never and always, I can honestly say that I NEVER once heard the mother speak to or about her daughters with kindness, warmth or respect. However, I all too frequently heard her ridicule them and blame them for the woes in her life. She almost always spoke to them in a nagging or hostile voice, and I had not once witnessed any show of physical affection toward any of her daughters. Actually, I looked hard and long for some semblance of warmth coming from this mother to her children, but I left Houston two years later without ever seeing any. There was clearly no joy for her in parenting these girls.

Through my conversations with her, I learned that her now estranged husband was openly disappointed that each of the three girls had not been a boy when they were born. As ridiculous as it seems, she said that he overtly blamed her for not producing offspring of the male gender, and subsequently took no part, other than financially, in parenting the children. I speculate that at some point the mother began to displace her anger at the husband onto her three vulnerable girls. (In psychological jargon, we call this *transference* - The transference of feelings occurs when we displace our feeling for one person [who we don't assess as safe] onto a person with whom we feel it is safe to express them.) Since the mom lacked the foresight to understand her own behavior, she developed a dreadful habit of blaming the girls for all of her unhappiness. My suspicion is that she was really angry with her husband and herself, but it was easier to blame the girls. To make matters worse, she had a very dysfunctional relationship with her own mother.

Looking back on this situation, I feel that had the mother been willing to reach out and seek support, she may have heard her children's horrific cries for help and gained the insight needed to develop compassion for her daughters and design a better attitude about parenting. When I last spoke to a former neighbor and inquired about this family, it appears that the situation had deteriorated further. The eldest daughter had left to live with the Aunt, and the youngest had been sent to an expensive boarding school for children with personality disorders.

The situation above is an extreme example of a lack of compassion for one's children and of joyless parenting. The real travesty is that there are many people, like my neighbor or Terrible Tiffany' parents who lack the awareness or perhaps the commitment to learn to understand the nature of children. I have met many people who believe that their children are more of a curse than a blessing, and few things have as profound an effect on a child's developing self-esteem as feeling a burden to one's parents. Even when parents say all the right things and discipline reasonably, if there is an undertone of discontent with family life, children grow up to feel that the parent's discontent is their fault and consequently grow to feel unworthy, undeserving and unlovable. Do any of you recognize this feeling?

When we take the time to understand why our children are behaving as they do, we gain compassion and understanding for them and for all of humanity. I urge you to observe your own level of compassion for your children. You might want to ask yourself if you truly take the time to listen to your children and try to understand what they might be thinking and feeling - particularly when they are misbehaving, crying, angry or sad. I am convinced that had my neighbor taken this level of care with her children, her children would have felt precious, loved and valued.

Had my neighbor also expressed warmth and genuine joy in parenting her daughters, things may have turned out quite differently as well. Warmth, like compassion is essential to a healthy home environment and healthy parent/child relationships. With respect to warmth in our homes, I urge you to treat your children as friends and also to **think** of your children as friends. I get a bit upset when I hear reputable family therapists and syndicated columnists insist that our children do not need us as friends, but need us instead as disciplinarians. Certainly we shouldn't allow them to get away with things that their friends might, and certainly we must be firm in enforcing our family rules and values, but our children should be our friends, because if we are lucky, we will be spending the rest of our lives in intimate relationship with them. A true friend is someone who displays warmth, honesty, compassion, respect and shared joy.

The characteristics above are all characteristics that a good parent should exhibit. When we honor our children as our friends, it makes it difficult to treat them as second class citizens or possessions. It would behoove us to remember what Kahlil Gibran says in the quote at the beginning of an earlier chapter, *"Our children come through us, not for us."* They belong to the Universe, not to us! They cannot be our possessions, but they can be our allies and loving companions. We as parents and teachers can be their mentors, their allies and their loving companions in return.

F. A Sense of Celebration - One of the greatest social skills we can possess is the quality of celebration and joy for life. People gravitate to those who live in joyful celebration. They are assessed by others as having "charisma."

In the *Confident Learner*, there is a list of the eight greatest hallmarks of a good parent. On the list was the ability to *Celebrate special moments with children, no matter how small.*[31] I completely agree. I also happen to subscribe to the belief that life is a wonderfully joyful celebration and is affirmed each time we celebrate the small, clear, joyous moments in our day to day lives.

A client of mine once stated that one of the biggest travesties of her childhood was the squelching of her enthusiasm by her parents. Words parents use to squelch excitement usually sound like: "Don't be getting yourself excited over nothing," "Don't get too excited, x,y and z hasn't happened yet," "Don't get too excited or you'll overheat yourself and get sick," or "Don't count your chickens before they hatch." Many of us who heard these suggestions when we became excited as children, grew up to lack enthusiasm and a sense of wonder as adults. Because I value quietness so dearly, at times I have found myself unintentionally squelching my children's loud enthusiasm as well. When I catch myself doing this, I often retract my statement and allow them to express their enthusiasm in constructive, fun and sometimes even loud ways.

I have another quote on my refrigerator that says;

> *Too often we look for spectacular excitement*
> *while we snub contentment.*

I think that in order to cultivate a sense of celebration for life and for our children, we must teach them through example how to spot, be thankful for and celebrate many of the simple pleasures that make life so sweet.

My children, my husband and I have developed the knack for turning fairly routine occasions into cause for celebration. We

---

[31] Author Unknown, "The Confident Learner," (Indiana: Grayson Bernard Publishing, 1992.)

celebrate the first day of daylight savings time, the first cold night of winter, A+'s in Math as well as hard earned C's in reading. Frankly we never get tired of making, as Shakespeare once said, *Much ado about nothing.* We also spend lots of fun time and energy planning celebrations, too. There are so many things in all of our lives to be thankful for and to celebrate. Each celebration is also in and of itself a perfect expression of gratitude for all the blessings that have been bestowed upon us each day. Father Matthew Fox once stated : "If the only prayers we ever said were prayers of thanksgiving , our prayers would be complete."

Exercise 32

Excluding the usual holidays, list 10 occasions you can celebrate with your family by doing something special. Describe what you might do.

Friday the 13th	**We can bake a black cat cake and tell stories of our funny misfortunes while celebrating all the good luck we have throughout the year.**
First day of spring	

I highly recommend the practice of joyful celebration in your home. If you are fortunate enough to have young children around, they can be excellent scouts and sources themselves for discovering reasons to celebrate. There is nothing more precious in life than a high-spirited individual, big or small, who enjoys the significance of simple pleasures, and with even the smallest amount of encouragement, kids do this wonderfully well. Actually, this is one area in which you can model your own behavior off our children's. Observe the joy in which they celebrate their day to day life experiences. Like when they jump and gyrate around the cracks in the sidewalk or the prance of delight when they put on a new pair of shoes. Strive also to restore your own *childhood sense of wonderment.* Or as many psychologists of today advise - take you inner child out to play.

The last major category of qualities that parents want their children to possess is:

III. INTEGRITY AND A HIGH STANDARD OF ETHICS

A. Ethics and Morals - As in everything else, the best way to instill ethics and morals in our children is by exhibiting those values, ethics and moral behaviors ourselves. Though peer pressure, television and advertisements can also have a serious impact on the value system of the developing person, often these impressions are not lasting ones. It is my contention that even when children from highly functional homes stray from the sound values of their parents, they often come full circle as adults and value those ethics and moral behaviors that their parents displayed to them as children. The moral behaviors and ethics that parents demonstrate are the ones that are much more likely to appear in their children, sooner or later, than those ethics and morals that parents may have preached but not practiced.

Several years ago my wise husband tried to reassure me of how strong our own moral influence was in our son's life. My son who was six-years-old at the time befriended a ten-year-old child who he met in the park one afternoon. This ten-year-old child who happened to live in our neighborhood, had some habits that rivaled those of the three girls in my previous story. This child also exhibited profound and pervasive symptoms of ADHD, Attention Deficit Hyperactivity Disorder. He was very restless, almost manic at times, bounced hastily from one activity to another and had a very low threshold for boredom. He also resorted to physical violence when he did not get his way. Because he lived on the next corner, he began coming to our home. Though I set and enforced strict limits when this child was around, I began to see some of the more undesirable behaviors cropping up in my son, Matthew.

On the day that I announced to my husband that I would no longer allow this ten year-old to visit our home, he questioned my judgment. Having heard from several sources that this boy's parents were very uninvolved in his life, my compassionate husband felt that we could be much more of a positive influence on him than he could be a negative influence on Matthew. He also reassured me that Matthew's misbehaviors were temporary, and that we would continue to provide, through example, the strongest models for his developing personality.

With strict supervision, I agreed to allow the boy to continue visiting. It was not long before my husband's prophecy came to pass. Matthew grew tired of the "bad habits" that he had picked up, probably because he grew tired of the natural and enforced consequences that came with them. He became his wonderful self-disciplined and kind self again. His new playmate even began to exhibit calmer, more polite, more focused behaviors when at our home.

This experience helped reassure me that parents really are the most important influence in the development of moral and ethical behavior. It also allowed me to see how influential we can be in the lives of other people's children as well. Even during the teen years, when peer pressure and peer influence are at their peak, children continue to look to their parents, especially if they are loving, accepting, supportive parents, for wisdom and guidance.

B. Honesty - If we value honesty as a characteristic we want present in our children, we must be honest with our children. We must be honest with others and we must be honest in our day to day dealings in life. Unfortunately, many parents expect complete honesty and integrity from their children, but fail to live up to those values themselves. I remember a friend of mine sitting at dinner once, bragging about cheating the IRS on his taxes. This man is a very nice man, and we love him dearly, but I think that to him and many others, cheating the IRS is a socially acceptable crime. At any rate, it was no longer than a month or two later that this same man was distraught and baffled by his son's impending college trial for cheating. I remember him exclaiming, "How could he do this to us? We taught him better than that." At that moment, I wondered how often his son had seen his father come home with office supplies or how often his son had to lie for him by telling a telephone caller that his father was not home. I also wondered if he had bragged to his son as he did to us about cheating the IRS. Acceptable behavior to many, but I wonder whether this man's somewhat subtle dishonesty was the catalyst for his son's decision to cheat on his test?

The point I am striving to make with this story is that children see things as black or white. If your child hears you lie to the encyclopedia salesman by telling him that you already have encyclopedias when you don't, then you are teaching your child, through example, that it is all right to lie, in order to get out of a tough or uncomfortable situation. Consequently, your child will learn to value lying when he gets in a jam and needs a solution.

Parents often lie to their children to make life a little easier. I must confess, I too have lied to my children to make my own life a little easier. If, for example, I wanted one of my children to stop crying for another ice cream cone, I might have told them that it was all gone. Sometimes I got away with this behavior, but if my child happened to look in the freezer later or see me eating some ice cream the next day, I was caught red handed, and the lie I told reinforced the value of lying when it's the easier way out.

If, however, you and I show our children that we are truthful, even when it produces mild to serious discomfort, our children will learn first hand, that tactful truthfulness is a virtue to be nourished. Stealing, cheating and lying are not instinctive behaviors. They must be taught and continually fostered. Honesty, truthfulness and integrity on the other hand, are inborn, natural ways of responding to the world around us. When you exhibit a high level of honesty, integrity and truthfulness yourself, you will foster these naturally occurring characteristics in your children as well.

C. **Charitability** - Giving to others who are less fortunate, who are in need, or to whom we simply want to give is not only a wonderful service to mankind, but is one of the most effective ways I know to enhance the state of mind or mood of both the giver and the receiver. As I mentioned earlier, I often recommend charity work to my clients, and I recommend that parents instill this social value in their children as well. I and many other social scientists encourage the virtue of generosity, because the antithesis of generosity, self-centeredness or egocentricity, is at the core of many mental dysfunctions and is of epidemic proportions in American society. Many mental dysfunctions can be prevented or cured if the individual is taught to develop aspects of his self-esteem through the virtue of a charitable action or giving of himself to others.

One of the greatest travesties of egocentricity is that the self-centered individual tends to magnify his own problems, because his sole focus is on himself. Charitability often takes the obsessive focus off the individual and draws the individual's attention to others who need him. In Gestalt philosophy, as well as in many other philosophical and religious trainings, turning one's attention toward social and global concerns is one of the highest states of existence an individual can achieve.

I have heard many behavioral scientists, philosophers and religious leaders speak on the topic of altruism. They all tend to agree that the value of altruism is limitless. Charity is a great panacea for both the giver and the receiver. Visible benefits result when the recipient is given the gift of another person's time, money, possessions, etc., and also from the knowledge that someone cares enough about them to help. The giver benefits as well from the act of feeling needed by another. Feeling needed by others automatically gives our life a sense of purpose and meaning, and according to Victor Frankl and several other great philosophers, the search for purpose and meaning is what motivates every action of our lives.

If you haven't done something significantly charitable lately or given someone an unexpected gift or performed a random act of kindness, I encourage you to go out and do so. For the act of giving of yourself makes us feel needed and creates a positive mood and sense of belonging in the world. It is also wonderful for our children to see us in charitable action. Let your children come up with ways of sharing of themselves as well. When we instill the value of charitability in our children, we give them a great gift. We create a space for them to develop a sense of communion with the world around them and allow them to learn and experience the wonderful emotional and often spiritual benefits of giving to others.

Exercise 33

List 5 random acts of kindness you will perform within the next two weeks

1. _____

2. _____

3. _____

4. _____

5. _____

D. Acceptance (or the lack of prejudice and judgment) - I feel that this value must be cultivated with much more diligence and with much more sincerity that it has been in the past. If our world is to truly heal and be a place where we can all live in peace, acceptance must be cultivated within ourselves and within our children with great rigor, vigilance and determination.

Being accepting and respectful flies in the face of convention. Historically and presently, our world is filled with moral "minority" groups who have the truth, the light and the way. The problem with this truth, light and way is that it leaves little room for us to have individual preferences. I am clear, however, that none of us ever set out to be judgmental or prejudiced toward others. Each of us are born with a whole and complete sense of unity with all that surrounds us. Yet we become prejudiced and judgmental because we are bombarded with racial and evaluative statements about our fellow man almost on a daily basis - Often in our very own homes. One of the most significant and telling traits of a fully functional human being or self-actualized person is their lack of prejudice or judgment against others.

All prejudice and judgment ultimately stem from a lack of understanding and respect for who we are as individuals. In other words, the truly self-confident individual has no need to bolster his ego by attacking or negating another's. He has a deep knowing that he, like all others, is worthy simply because he exists. He consequently accepts others for who and what they are, because he has no need or desire to elevate himself above others through prejudice and moral judgment.

I love to quote the prophetic Dr. Wayne Dyer. In a lecture given at Unity Church in Houston, Texas, he assessed judgment as follows.

When we judge others, we do not define them,
but define ourselves by our own need to judge.

What this quote speaks to me, is that when we devalue others through harsh judgment or prejudice, we are speaking our own hidden fears and insecurities. For if we weigh the worth of others, we must also be weighing the worth of ourselves. The truly enlightened being knows that an individual's worth cannot be measured and is a grace given from God without any expectation in return. As the phrase goes, "We are worthy simply because we exist." So the task of weighing one's self-worth through criticism or prejudice against others is self-defeating as well as crippling to our relationships with the world around us.

We must strive as enlightened parents, to become aware of our own judgments, criticisms and prejudices. We must also learn to become more accepting of our fellowman whatever their preferences, lifestyles or characteristics. When we embrace acceptance of others, we will gain the freedom and the wisdom to value our own self-worth without measurement against another. When our children grow up in an environment of acceptance and love for all mankind, they learn to live peacefully within the world around them and learn to value their own self-worth without measurement. When all parents and children have risen to this level of total acceptance and immeasurable self-worth, we will become a world of self-actualized, peaceful, loving individuals. I implore you to begin today to teach acceptance and love to those you love, and your world will become a truly magnificent place. The price we pay for prejudice and non-acceptance is resentment, isolation, violence and war.

In closing, all of the behaviors and attributes that have been mentioned are aspects of our personalities that are most highly influenced by the suggestive power of observation. To put it in more general terms, parents, teacher, counselors, etc. show children how to develop their attributes and behaviors through example. Exemplary, or modeled behavior is the most effective way to teach the developing child. Parents and other individuals who are in influential positions must develop a keen awareness of the impact their own behaviors and attitudes have upon the developing mind. If we all take this responsibility seriously, and lovingly accept our roles as mentors, then we can inspire a new generation of peaceful, ambitious, joyful, accepting, respectful, loving people - Generations of individuals who will elevate our precious earth to the level of consciousness and peacefulness she deserves.

What Parents Want for Their Children

I. Emotional Well-Being
A. Self-Confidence
B. Freedom from Neurotic Tendencies
C. Balance
D. Joy and Peacefulness
E. Success
F. Freedom from Addictions

II. Social Skills
A. The Ability to Develop Intimate Relationships with Others
B. Eye Contact and Attentiveness to Others
C. "Common" Courtesy
D. Peaceful Conflict Resolution
E. Warmth and Compassion
F. A Sense of Joy and Celebration

III. High Standards of Integrity
A. Ethics and Morals
B. Honesty
C. Charitability
D. Acceptance

All of childhood's unanswered questions
must finally be passed back
to the town and answered there.
Heroes and bogey men, values and dislikes,
are first encountered and labeled in that
early environment.

"I Know Why the Caged Bird Sings" - Maya Angelou

Chapter 16

Concluding Remarks

At the conclusion of this book, I sit in retrospect, hoping that my mission has been accomplished. My purpose in writing this book was to support others in realizing how precious our children are to us and the important impact that mood, conversation and action has upon all their lives.

In verbal conversation, it is vital and essential to the healthy development of our children to administer words of acknowledgment, encouragement, admiration and respect. At the same time, it is crucial to eliminate the negative suggestions that set children up for failure.

In our non-verbal conversation and in what we model, it is imperative that we communicate the moods, actions and beliefs that provide our children with the most nourishing and life-enhancing examples possible. Hugs, smiles, laughter and gestures of approval are several of the many effective, positive non-verbal communication skills that empower children to develop healthy self-confidence, self-respect and love and concern for others.

By now I trust that you realize that all of the exercises and suggestions that I presented can also apply to your relationship with yourself and with the other significant individuals in your life, like your husband, wife, boss, mother, father, brother, sister, co-worker, neighbor, friend and foe.

When using the techniques and suggestions that I have presented in this book, I ask that you take into consideration the following:

1. **Practice, practice and more practice produces competency.**
2. **Recognizing and acknowledging yourself for your best efforts encourages continued growth.**
3. **Setbacks are opportunities for reflection and growth.**
4. **Almost anything done long enough will become a habit.**

There may be days when you seem to have forgotten to use the positive parenting skills that you acquired in reading this book and from other parenting sources. At those times it is especially important for you to focus on the four rules on the previous page. On any given day, there will be many things that you did right as a parent. Reinforce these positive actions by acknowledging them. Also learn from your mistakes, but don't torment yourself with guilt and shame over them. I promise you that it's O.K. to be human. We all are. As a friend of mine once said, "If we weren't supposed to make mistakes, we would have been given wings."

There are times when in the process of establishing good habits, individuals allow themselves to sabotage their valiant efforts with one lapse of old behavior. Take dieting for example. Many individuals who go on a restrictive diet, feel like complete failures when they eat a forbidden food. Consequently their failure leads them to "blow" or call off the whole diet because of this one slip up. They forget all the days that they dieted successfully and focus on the one that they did not. Often times a simple candy bar or bag of chips can send a dieter into a downward spiral. The sad truth is that there is no power or magic in a candy bar or bag of chips. At it's worst a big bag of chips is only about 1,000 calories and a really big box of candy about 2,000. This won't even register a pound on the scale, but the dieter viewing this as a major setback, feels morally defeated and reverts back to old comfortable patterns.

I urge you to view your developing parenting skills, not as an all or nothing proposition, but as a slow, steady progression toward healthy habits. There will be many backslides into old habits. Be gentle with yourself as you learn. Keep adding on to your new skills. Persevere. Be willful, focused and rigorous about establishing healthy, life-enhancing parenting skills. Your children are worth the effort. Creating an atmosphere where an individual can learn to live life well, is the most important thing we can ever do in this lifetime.

Establishing lasting habits takes time, practice and patience. An essential key to maintaining the new skills that you've learned is to reward yourself when you notice that you have been using them. On the days when you have taken a step backward, be gentle with yourself and take note of the two steps that you have taken forward. Remember the subconscious mind likes to avoid conflict and change, so it pushes back against change and new patterns, by providing us with opportunities to revert back to the familiar (no brainer) ones. If you revert back to less effective parenting habits, acknowledge yourself for noticing them, get excited about noticing them - remembering that awareness is 90% of the cure, and remind yourself that you are in the process of transcending those old behavioral or mood patterns and actively, consciously developing healthier ones.

As parents, you will have many moments and days of truly inspired parenting, so honor yourself by celebrating those, and remember to count them in your blessings at night. Rest assured that there will be other days when you are not at your parental best, and remember you are not alone - All of us, even people who write parenting books, have bad parenting days. No matter what kind of day you've had, if you stay mindful of what you have done right, you will continue to make forward strides.

In almost every month, there is at least one or two irritable days where I tend to lose my temper, nag, whine or bark orders at my children. Though I am taking actions to handle my mood swings more effectively, I am also learning to have compassion for myself during these times.

During these off periods, I find it helpful to reassure my family that they are not to blame for my less than sunny moods. Consequently, my husband and children are becoming very tolerant of me on these days, and at times they are even sympathetic. My willingness to be honest with my family teaches them three valuable distinctions. 1) To be loving and accepting of another family member when they are in the throws of a "bad" mood. 2) That it's okay to be irritable, sad, angry and grouchy on occasion and, 3) That other's moods come and go and we shouldn't take them so personally.

Someday I may find a way to tackle the emotional joy ride of PMS before I begin menopause, but at least for now my family knows my "Don't touch me, talk to me or I'll jump out of my skin" moods are my own issues, and did not result from something they did. In these moments, I also remember to reassure myself that my dark moods will surely pass and with or without them, I am still a lovable, loving person.

Just last week I received a big payoff for being a conscientious as well as a conscious parent. My family and I were out for a long drive when I nonchalantly asked my son Matthew if he would like to have himself as his own best friend. After hearing the question, he made a facial expression that suggested the answer to the question should have been obvious to me. After a brief pause he replied, "Of course I would be my own best friend, because I'm my kind of guy!"

At that moment Matt's father John and I looked at each other and smiled deep and satisfying smiles. As we did, I could feel my heart fill with an overwhelming sense of accomplishment. I suspect John's did too. We knew that we had, in part, been responsible for Matthew's deep sense of self-acceptance and healthy self-esteem. This feeling of accomplishment however, is still fairly new to me, for in the past I had focused more on what I did wrong than what I did right. I am happy to say that acknowledging my own honor and dignity as a person and mother is becoming easier as time goes by. I sincerely hope that I have planted the seeds for you to recognize and honor your own gifts as a person and as a parent as well.

In conclusion, I would like you to acknowledge yourself for completing this book. I am fairly confident that those who choose to read this book are already ambitious and deeply loving parents.

I say this with confidence, because I know that most individuals who read parenting and other self-help books are confident in their life's skills but not complacent and continue to seek better tools for living. They tend to be truly committed to their children and to their children's healthy growth and success in life.

You are also in the process of achieving what many parents and individuals have not yet begun to pursue - The wisdom and courage to be a five star inspiration in the lives of your children or anyone who you choose to inspire through your positive attitude, words and actions. You have the keys; now unlock the doors to a joyful, healthy, inspired existence for yourself and for your loved ones.

As you pass these distinctions on to your children, watch how many other doors open along the way. It is a wonderful rippling effect, and for each life that you touch with the power of positive suggestion, many lives will be touched in return. Love, peace and harmony are within your reach. Go ahead and celebrate your life. Your are doing well, so continue on this marvelous path of discovery. Discover as many wonderful treasures and opportunities as you can. The world is composed of an infinite amount of them and beckons you to design the life you want for you and your children. When you design it through a positive mood and though positive conversations you can never go wrong.

I agree with Whitney Houston when she sings; *I believe the children are our future, teach them well and let them lead the way.* I believe that "teaching them well" means teaching them through our own positive example and by our positive words, actions and attitudes that reflect life as a cup to be filled - not emptied -- A cup that can overflow with happiness, peace and harmony for each and every one of us.

Blessings and light to you. Namaste, *Tamyra*

BIBLIOGRAPHY

Reference **Page #**

Albert Ellis, *A New Guide To Rational Living*, (Hollywood: Wilshire   41, 44
Book Company, 1975)

Wayne Dyer, *Your Erroneous Zones* (New York: Funk and Wagnalls,   44
1976)

National Geographic Magazine, Vol.192, No.3 September 1997   75

Thich Nhat Hanh, *Peace is Every Step* (New York: Bantam Books,   76
1991)

Wayne Dyer, *What Do You Really Want for Your Kids?* (New York: 79
William Morrow, 1985)

Harold S. Kushner, *How Good Do We Have to Be* (New York: 97
Random House, 1996)

Carl Covitz, *Emotional Child Abuse* (Boston: Sego Press, 1991) p. 10.   125

Frank Taylor, *The Pleasure of Their Company* (Radnor: Chilton,   126
1981) p. 151

ECaP, 1302 Chapel St. New Haven, Conn. 06511 (203) 865-8392   131

Candace Pert, Ph.D., The Center for Molecular and Behavioral   132
Neuroscience, Rutgers University.

Charles Boudin, *Suggestion and Auto Suggestion* (New York: Dodd,   133
Mead Publishing, 1922)

The Journal of Alternative Medicine, Paryallup, WA: Future   139
Medicine Publishing, Inc., p. 72.

Tourovues, "Hypnosis: The Healing Power of Suggestion," New   140
Orleans, La.

Reference	Page #
Frank Taylor, *The Pleasure of Your Company* (Radnor: Chilton, 1981), p. 165.	150
Elizabeth Barrett Browning, *Sonnets From the Portuguese*	150
Vince Napoli, *Adjustment and Growth* (St. Paul: West Publishing, 1985), p. 87-88.	160
Adele Faber and Elaine Mazlish, *Siblings Without Rivalry* (New York: Avon Books, 1987)	163
Alice Miller, *For Your Own Good* (New York: Farrar Straus, 1983), p. 140	177
Vicki Lansky, *101 Ways to Make Your Child Feel Special* (Chicago, Comtempo, 1991)	178, 210
H. Jackson Brown, *Life's Little Instruction Book* (Nashville: Ruthledge Hill, 1991), p. 373.	210
John Roger and Peter McWilliams, *You Can't Afford The Luxury of a Negative Thought* (Los Angeles: Prelude Press, 1991), pp. 277-288.	218
Jerry Wyckoff, Ph.D., and Barbara C. Unell, *Without Spanking or Spoiling* (New York: Simon and Schuster, 1984)	241
Robert Firestone, *Compassionate Child Rearing* (New York: Plenum Press, 1990)	251
Ralph Waldo Emerson, Origin of Quote Unknown.	270
Education For Living Seminars, 3113 Ryan Street, Suite 3, Lake Charles, Louisiana 70601, 1(888) 335-7952	276
Author Unknown, "The Confident Learner," (Indiana: Grayson Bernard Publishing, 1992.)	276

If you would like additional copies of this book, please order by choosing one of the three following options:

1.) Call (225) 753-1452,
2.) Send orders to the address below. Make checks payable to Tamyra Bourgeois in the amount of $18.00 plus $5.00 for postage.
3.) Visit our website: tbourgeois.com

Thank you.

**Tamyra Bourgeois, Ph.D
4606 Jones Creek Road Suite 130
PMB 135
Baton Rouge, La. 70817-1527**

Book Order Form

Name_____phone(___)_____

Address_____

City, St. Zip_____

Number of books_____ Amount of check_____

NOTES